My Dartmoor

Clive Gunnell

Introduced by
JEREMY THORPE M.P.

BOSSINEY BOOKS

*First published in 1977
by Bossiney Books
St Teath, Bodmin, Cornwall
Typeset and printed in Great Britain by
Penwell Ltd, Parkwood, Callington,
Cornwall*

For Michael who had the courage
to launch me on this great adventure
called writing.

CONTENTS

LIST OF PLATES

(Pages 57-68)

Even today Dartmoor, in a curious way, can seem more remote than the faces of the moon.

The Moor is, of course, a world of its own. Clive Gunnell though knows it well. His three hundred-year-old cottage, just outside Tavistock, in which he wrote this book, has distant glimpses of the tors. So Dartmoor, in a real sense, is the window of his world. When a man, walking across this landscape, can write: 'I am alone. I am king. I have all this,' we know he has a special quality. Inside these pages he invites us to share experience — and to widen our vision and understanding, not only of the Moor, but of ourselves.

Those, who have seen Clive Gunnell's immensely talented Westward TV walks and programmes about the Westcountry, will know of his ability to inspire. He encourages us to get out of the car, and start exploring for ourselves. Whereas when a TV programme ends, we have only a memory, in this, his first book we have a permanent guideline to aspects of the Moor. But MY DARTMOOR is no mere guidebook. This is a mixture of the man and the region; the men and women who live and work here; the animals and birds who equally people it.

Enjoy it, explore it and appreciate it.

Clive Gunnell encourages us to do just that.

INTRODUCTION

Codden Beacon is the highest point in North Devon. Choose a clear moment just before rain, or on a crisp cloudless day in winter, or a soft warm summer's evening when the heat haze has lifted, and a vast patchwork of Westcountry splendour will unroll before you: the great ridge that is Exmoor; Hangman Hill above Combe Martin; Lundy, squatting like some mallard duck twenty miles out into the Atlantic; Hartland Point sticking like a great finger into the sea; Bodmin Moor over forty miles away to the South West; Dartmoor, and the hills which hide Exeter. The view is at its most dramatic when winter caps Exmoor, Dartmoor and Bodmin Moor simultaneously with peaks of snow.

But whatever the season the frontiers of Dartmoor where Okehampton is the outpost, will for me always be the Himalayas: the great mountain range cutting off my prying gaze from the lush plains of lowland Devon, as if guarding Torquay and Dartmouth, Kingsbridge and Plymouth from an invasion from the North.

Exmoor I know and love. To Dartmoor I am a stranger and respectful. And even when driving to Plymouth from North Devon one is careful only to skirt the Moor travelling by Sourton and Blackdown, Horrabridge and Yelverton.

In this book like some grand finale in a firework display Clive Gunnell tenderly illuminates each place that he loves: Trowlesworthy Warren and Prewley Moor; Langcombe Brook and Pupers Hill, Shavercombe Moor and Broada Falls; Gibby Combe Wood and Scorriton Down. Each conveys a sense of magic and mystery.

But Dartmoor has always been worked by man. The Tin Streamers in the thirteenth century gave way to the Peat Workers and Warreners in the nineteenth; the Clay Workers in the early twentieth century and today, almost alone, the Farmer. The granite for London Bridge came from Merrivale, just as the granite for the embankment came from my own constituency Island, Lundy; there are the remains of the Gunpowder Factory and Powder Mills and the Ice Factory at Prewley Moor.

Dartmoor, too, has produced rich personalities. Robert Herrick of Dean Prior; Charles Kingsley of Holne; Wallace Perryman, whose farm was probably the first in Britain to have (and still have) electricity powered by water wheel. He tells of his grandfather, the Parish Constable, who would walk a convicted prisoner handcuffed the eighteen miles to Exeter prison, returning himself again on foot; William Palmer, who saved England by ensnaring ravens at Sourton thereby averting the curse that would fall on England if the ravens at the Tower of London should become extinct. Since at that time only one raven had survived, it was, as the Duke of Wellington would say, 'The nearest run thing you ever saw in your life.'

For the present day my vote is for the hospitality of Mrs Mudge, the chatelaine of the Drewe Arms at Drewsteignton who has presided there for the past fifty seven years.

The challenge of politics has not been absent. Following the dissolution of the Joint Stannary Parliaments of Devon and Cornwall in 1305, the Parliament of Dartmoor Tin Miners met in 1494. By the reign of Henry VIII in 1512 they deemed themselves powerful enough to challenge the Mother of Parliaments itself. Displeased with the M.P. for Plympton, Richard Strode, for daring to introduce a bill to prevent the blocking of harbours by refuse from the stream works, they ordered him to appear before them on Crockern Tor, and upon refusal threw him into Lydford Castle, described by Parliament as 'one of the most hainous, contagious, and detestable places in the realm'. He languished there a month and was not released until he posted a bond for £100 with the deputy warden of the Stannaries. It was only when Strode's Act was passed by Westminster followed by the abolition of some privileges and the curtailment of others that the

Stannary Parliament was finally curbed. Judge Jefferies of the Bloody Assizes held his Court in Lydford Castle and the phrase is still current in West Devon: 'Lydford Law, or hang first and try afterwards.'

Historically the whole of Devon and Cornwall was afforested by the Normans, and thereby subject to the Sumptuary Laws. The only places which remained free of such Royal restrictions were the prosperous Saxon Boroughs of Barnstaple and Totnes. By 1240 King John, critically short of money, agreed for cash to release all of Devon, save for Exmoor and Dartmoor. On the benefit side all ratepayers in Devon save for those in Barnstaple and Totnes may enpasture their cattle on the Moors — although now with the advent of the Commons Registration Act they have got to prove their credentials first. As the Member for Barnstaple we do not object to this preferential treatment provided we can continue to explore the mysteries of Dartmoor.

In recent years Dartmoor has inspired and I suspect will continue to inspire many a battle, involving the army, the Water Authority, the Conservationists and the farming community. Perhaps we should re-elect the Stannary Parliament to maintain the balance, provided, of course, they do not seek once again to usurp the sovereignty of the Parliament at Westminster. Here perhaps is an agreed case for devolution.

For my part, I agree with Cicero that one 'flies from the town to the country as though from chains'. Nowhere is that truer than with the glories of our County of Devon, chief of which are Dartmoor and Exmoor, the twin jewels in the crown.

Jeremy Thorpe

February 1977

I

DISCOVERING DARTMOOR

No doubt you sometimes almost loathe the sun. And yet, you know, I should like to feel the full force of it again, burning the skin and making the whole frame glow, and reminding me that I have still got a body. If only I could get tired of the sun, instead of books and thoughts. I should like to have my animal's existence awakened, not the kind that degrades a man, but the sort that delivers him from the stuffiness and spuriousness of a purely intellectual existence, and makes him purer and happier. Modern sun-worship is romantic nonsense. It gets intoxicated over the sunrise and sunset. It knows something about the power of the sun, but does not know it as a reality, but only as a symbol. It cannot understand the way the ancients worshipped it as a God.

Dietrich Bonhoeffer
Letters and Papers from Prison

These words were written by a man who was never again allowed the joy and freedom of experiencing the force of the sun. Less than a year after he wrote them he was hanged by the Gestapo at Flassenburg.

Dietrich Bonhoeffer was a Christian Martyr, his *Letters from Prison* scribbled on scraps of paper and smuggled out to his parents and friends by humani tarian jail guards, are the most moving documents of my lifetime. They have the power to stimulate the reader with strength to face life, and give joy in the appreciation of it.

It may seem strange to open a book about Dartmoor with a quotation from a German Pastor executed by his own countrymen for his opposition to Hitler; but I can only excuse it by explaining the circumstances surrounding my discovery of that passage.

Some years ago I left my cottage, on the outskirts of Tavistock, and journeyed into Dartmoor to Cadover Bridge. At that time there was much speculation concerning the Countryside Commission's proposed Plymouth-Lynmouth Bridleway, the idea being to establish a route open to walkers and riders from the outskirts of Plymouth across Dartmoor, Central Devon, Exmoor and in to Lynton and Lynmouth. Many routes had been discussed but none finalised. The creation of such a pathway appealed to me and I decided to try and walk my own route, beginning with Dartmoor. I set myself no time limits, and was prepared to deviate from my course at any time to view something interesting or different, or merely to obtain a better vantage point for enjoying the scenic grandeur surrounding me. I chose a route from Plymouth that took me through the Plym Forest to Shaugh Prior and from there an easy walk to the China Clay world at Lee Moor, and on to Cadover Bridge.

I have always been fascinated by the attraction this area around Cadover Bridge holds for Plymouthians. On almost every fine day in the summer it is jammed with cars, the occupants sitting on the banks of the Plym picnicking, watching the children damming the water, paddling, or walking along the sandy fringes with fishing-nets, scooping into jars anything that wriggles, hops or swims.

I have heard many, with that self-appointed superiority that one class can effect concerning another, ask, 'Why do they do it? They have the whole of Dartmoor to play on — why do they choose this place?' Indeed, I wondered myself why this spot was so important to so many, but as in most things, the answer is simple. Children love water. They need water and seek it as a playground wherever they live, whatever their environment. Plymouth may well be one of the most famous and important ports in British history, but it does not have an abundance of sandy beaches and those on its fringes are not easily accessible, nor are they always safe for children. Dartmoor may contain two enormous blanket bogs that give birth to and feed its fourteen rivers, but the pools fit for bathing created on their way to the sea are known only to a handful of dedicated walkers — and there are no lakes. The reservoirs provide open water but without exception forbid paddling and swimming, so where else can they go? Cadover is safety for the children and rest and relaxation for the parents who, without having to leave the verges of the Cornwood-Cadover road, can bask in the sun and watch the children. Later in life these same children, nurtured in this environment, can be met tramping the moor in all seasons, soaking in its history, beauty and mystery.

On this summer morning however, Cadover was deserted and not a human stirred as I left the Bridge behind. I crossed Trowlesworthy Warren and climbed Great Trowlesworthy Tor. It was my intention to walk from here to the village of Scorriton, a distance of roughly fourteen miles, taking me across one of the loneliest stretches of South Dartmoor, travelling an area unknown to me. Hen Tor Warren to Shavercombe Tor where the Cairn would point me towards Langcombe Head, and then Erme Head. From there I could take a bearing towards Huntingdon Warren and crossing the Western Walla Brook, walk across Buckfastleigh Moor to Scorriton Down and Scorriton.

To ensure my survival I wore stout walking boots laced to support my ankles and waterproofed, for however dry the summer I would cross large areas where I could sink at least ankle deep in mire and I would be skirting the limits of the Southern Morass. I carried a well-tested anorak, for I would climb above the low cloud level which in seconds envelop the walker in cold, clinging mist, chilling the bones and completely disorientating any sense of direction. Over my shoulder was slung a canvas duffle bag large enough to carry food and drink — in this case a bottle of white wine — for I know no greater pleasure than drinking wine chilled in a moorland stream in the solitude and peace of the open countryside and it has both medicinal and therapeutic qualities. In addition the bag contained two two-and-a-half inch to the mile Ordnance Survey maps of the area SX 66 and SX 56, and just in case, the one-inch to the mile map of the whole of Dartmoor. Finally a small pocket compass and two spare pairs of woollen socks. This is my standard equipment for walking the Moor, whatever the distance. Only in winter do I supplement it by wearing woollen shirts, and carrying a roll-neck seaman's jersey. Two other items I must mention: a walking stick (I now boast a fine collection), finding it invaluable over the rough terrain and although our Dartmoor cattle are the most placid of beasts, devoid of latent aggression towards the human race, you may always meet that odd one who likes to be different! In dire emergencies I can always rely on the assistance of my travelling companion, Thurber, a black Labrador bitch of limitless courage and endurance, possessing an infallible sense of direction home, from any distance and in any conditions, the moment I give the command 'Dinner!'.

My companion is well ahead of me, every fibre of her being glowing with animal content at the freedom of the morning, snuffling and sniffing at tuft and burrow, shooting away like 'a long dog' at the slightest whisper and in mock panic jack-knifing backwards to return and apologise for forgetting me. Without warning, meadow pipits rise skywards from the heather, alarmed at her approach, their strident 'pheet' striking discord in the silence until, at the peak of their climb, they glide earthwards triple-tonguing in perfect harmony.

The sun hidden behind the western heights at day's beginning climbs slowly above Brent Moor, burning off the shadows clinging to the sheltered slopes in a blanket of dark ruby. Its resuscitating breath soaks into the warm purple carpet where the dawn dew hangs in pearl clusters begging for a few seconds more of life in the splendour of their setting. The whole moorland is alive with colour, not harsh or garish but subdued in tones that embrace the whole range of the spectrum.

The interweaving patterns of heather contrast in purple hue through age, the new-born rich red fades to a gentler tone in middle life and at old age takes on the complexion of old port. In between the heathers the burnt out grass reflects the sunlight in burnished gold and isolated patches of whortleberries blaze scarlet against the brown. Away in the distance the granite-capped Tors now bathed in merciless light reflect back in blistering greys that sparkle and glitter in the brilliance.

Thurber has stopped her pointless darting hither and thither and settled to the tireless lope she could manage all day if required. Only occasionally does she disappear into the ling to reappear with tongue dripping water from some secret place. We are in harmony with the world.

Climbing a wall I leapt down almost on top of the largest dog fox I have ever seen sleeping in the wall's shade. More annoyed than frightened, he slowly uncurled, sweeping his brush at me in silent contempt and deliberately strolled away, turning his head once to flash back at me with angry, shining eyes for disturbing his slumber. Not even the presence of Thurber appearing by my side, after finding a suitably sized hole in the wall, could hurry the fox out of its leisured stride. Thurber obviously experiencing the same awe and excitement as I, made soft whining noises expectantly, but as I said nothing, she sat and waited for me to move on. Suddenly, deep in the heather where the fox had retired, five ravens rose in flight and began a slow circle overhead. Investigating, I found a sheep dead but a few hours and partly eaten. Was this the lunch he had been sleeping off? Where had he caught it? I had seen few sheep since Trowlesworthy Warren. Only hunger would drive them to search these heights for food at this time of the year. There were still rich pickings lower down. Puzzled, I continued walking and allowed the ravens to finish their meal.

Between us we had covered a lot of ground, and always climbing to the sun, Hen Tor to Shavercombe Head. Here it changed and became marsh which trembled underfoot as though it were well-sprung, adding buoyancy to my stride. Langcombe Head, where the brook rises almost in the shadow of Grimms grave on its right bank, with his kistvaen, or burial place, in the centre of a stone circle. With the sun a blazing beacon overhead, I journeyed towards Erme Head, picking up the Abbot's Way at Erme Pits Ford, and followed the route to Red Lake. The sweat trickled down by back and I opened my shirt, baring my body to the heat. Thurber had chosen a cooler path along the river bed and was exhibiting paroxysms of joy, exploding plumes of water into shimmering rainbows at every bound.

I paused at Red Lake to explore, for I was surrounded by all the debris of Dartmoor's industrial history. Here, over seven centuries ago the early tin streamers came searching for alluvial tin, building rough stone shelters from the abundance of granite boulders scattered around them. A shelf above their heads, probably sealed by a stone, protected their food from prowling wolves, and in the fireplaces they burned bracken and perhaps peat, for there were no trees for fuel. Throughout the long wet winter they cowered behind these inadequate, draughty walls for protection from the icy blasts that froze their blood, transforming joints and sinew into creaking, pain-wracked encumbrances that ached and protested every action of the body. Always, they worked with water. Their hands permanently immersed until the swollen knuckles forbade movement between the fingers. Grinding down the small stones between granite mill stones, washing it through layers of turf to separate the ore from the soil, and finishing off with a large wooden vessel, gently slopping away the residue until only ore remained. Isolated, lonely men, living in this fashion for months at a time, only occasionally tramping the rough tracks home to

their families on the moorland fringes. How they must
have prayed for winter's end, their chilled bodies
anticipating with eager longing that first soft touch of
summer's sun. These men and their lives were everywhere about me. At my feet the hole where the tin was
melted by building a fire over the top. There the
remains of a blowing house where later generations of
miners built a furnace fanned to white heat by wood
and leather bellows powered by a water wheel, driven
by the falling water from a hand cut leat.

I sat down on a granite mould stone into which the
ingots were cast and thought about these unknown
men, and was filled with a great sadness. What did it
benefit them, this enforced loneliness? What joy was
derived from toil that continued without respite until
it either killed them or they were so crippled in body by
the climatic excesses of their environment, they were
forced to charity in order to survive. As they laboured,
they were used and abused, cheated and robbed, and
yet they continued in this manner, emptying the moor
of its mineral wealth for five hundred years.

After the miners had gone it became the turn of a
new breed of men to scar the moor, at Red Lake. These
workers sliced up the turf above the granite, stacked it
and left it to dry. They were the peat workers who
arrived here in 1847 to cut peat for the naptha factory
at Shipley Bridge. In order to transport the peat a
tramway was built from Zeal Tor up to Red Lake. The
old shelters of the tin streamers were refurbished, and
the workers settled down to stamp their mark upon the
industrial surface of Dartmoor. They, also, worked in
isolation, using the tramway to transport their supplies.
This was, however, a short-lived occupation, for in
1855 the naptha factory closed leaving Red Lake and
its surroundings to return to the wild. The moor re-
possessed its own for over fifty years and then in 1905
Charles Cottier, a wealthy Plymouth solicitor and
property owner, cast his eyes around, seeking further
ways of amassing sums of money. He noticed that the
firm of Martin Brothers were becoming prosperous

from their profits made out of china clay, particularly from their pits at Lee Moor on the fringe of Dartmoor. He engaged R. Hansford Worth, Mineralogist, Civil Engineer and Dartmoor Recorder and Historian, to prospect for clay. After much searching he found appreciable clay beds at Red Lake where the deposit had been left exposed by the streamers' old workings. The size of Worth's discovery — depth of clay, sixty feet; area, six hundred yards by two hundred yards — was sufficient to encourage Cottier to develop the site. He formed a Company, the China Clay Corporation Limited, to work Red Lake and took into partnership two other men, Mallaby Deeley, founder of the Forty Shilling Tailors' chain of shops, and Charles Hanson, owner of Yorkshire woollen mills. Worth was commissioned to design and supervise the installation of the necessary machinery. From Ivybridge to Red Lake a three foot gauge tramway was laid, starting at Western Beacon around Weatherdon Hill, passing Hangershell Rock, Spurrell's Cross, Hobajons Cross, and then winding around Piles Hill, Sharp Tor and Three Barrows Hill. It avoided Knatta Burrow around Quickbeam Hill. On to Crossways and finally across the moor to Red Lake. This twisting, tortuous route was deliberately chosen for the clay left Red Lake by means of a gravity fed pipe-line laid with the track. Had the pipe-line been laid over the hills it would have meant pumping the clay its full length. This route added nearly four extra miles to the pipe-line.

Worth designed and built an engine house for a gas suction engine to provide power for the electric pumps. Half a mile from Red Lake, he laid out a mica separation plant at Greenhill mine and at Bittaford, close to the tramway terminus at Western Beacon; the clay dries were built and an inclined cableway erected to transport the product. By 1912 the whole project began operating, but two years later when war broke out, the pit was closed for the duration.

Cottier re-opened the pit for one year after the war and then sold out lock, stock and barrel for a paltry

£47,000 to the now Sir Mallaby Deeley, M.P. who had been knighted for his services to the tailoring trade.

The workings prospered under Deeley. He opened up the disused pit at Leftlake along the Erme valley, and his workers became an integrated part of the Dartmoor landscape. Once again the tin streamers' shelters were put to use, for these men also lived out here, often for months at a time. They cultivated small plots of land, growing vegetables to supplement the food sent up to them on the tramway.

In 1809 John Michelmore had obtained a ninety-nine year lease on Huntingdon Warren from the Duchy, on undertaking to enclose six hundred acres to create a warren. The aftermath of his efforts, over a hundred years later, was to provide the clay workers of Red Lake with a source of red meat, to break the monotony of their diet.

They caught rabbits by going out at night after they finished work and stretching nets across the open ground in front of the entrance to the burrows. At dawn, the rabbits, after their night's search for food, were driven into the nets by the workers and their dogs. To ensure a constant supply of rabbits for his workers, Deeley ordered artificial 'burys', the old Dartmoor name for burrows, to be made. This was a matter of digging a long trench with alternating branches leading off from each side, the whole covered with turf, and soil thrown over the top. Into these 'burys' pairs of breeding rabbits were introduced, and, as was the nature of the beast, the supply always exceeded the demand.

In this manner work continued at Red Lake for many years, but the economic slump of the twenties affected the sales of china clay, and smaller and smaller quantities were produced, until, as the thirties began, the tonnage from Red lake reached the lowest ever. In 1932 both Red Lake and Leftlake pits ceased production altogether and were offered for auction. Nobody was prepared to take the financial risk of leasing the pits, and so the whole works were put up for sale. The pump engines were sold individually, and the buildings

Worth had built to house them, blown up. Only the tramway remained for a few years longer and then was ripped up and sold for scrap. With the going of the rail, a whole era came to an end. This small area of Dartmoor had for centuries provided employment. Tough, and ill-paid, admittedly, but nevertheless a living for the working man. Now it ended. Miner, warrener, peat worker, clay worker, all gone and their going heralded the beginning of the end for the working man on Dartmoor. He only exists today on the moorland fringes in isolated pockets constantly sniped at by conservationists. It is possible to walk the moor for a week and never meet a working man. Only the occasional Range Rover loaded high with hay for some isolated herd indicates the presence of the only working community left on Dartmoor — the farmer.

I climbed the tramway embankment and headed towards the pit workings. As I walked, the air was alive with the sounds of these men. The creaking cables, clattering of trucks, the ringing peal of pick and shovel striking sparks against rock. The shouts and oaths. Who were these men? Unrewarded in life, unnoticed in death, they stamped their personality on the moor, gave it guts and character, fertilised it with their blood and sweat. Whilst they lived and worked they gave the moor vitality and humanity; without them it is a characterless museum.

I dwell upon what may appear to be trifles, small details, small people, because for me they hold a great significance. They were my education, and we learn from trifles. The things that are taught us by Shakespeare and Tolstoy only touch the surface of our minds. It is the trifles of life that penetrate to the heart, like dust into velvet, some- times poisoning it, sometimes ennobling it.Which is just why I feel like talking about good little people. The big ones may tell their own story. It is these others, living their quiet, unknown lives, who fade away without a sign, remembered by

nobody, and denied the great gesture. Yet these
people loved, and beauty was accessible to them.
They too, longed for the good life . . .

Chaliapin/Gorki

With the sun boring into my skull, my feet hot and
aching, I decided to rest and eat. I chose one of the
most magnificent locations on this stretch of moorland. Half a mile away from the clay workings the river
Avon (Aune) plunges and sweeps around a large
boulder-strewn bend and forms a cataract known as
Broad or Broada Falls. In the peaceful splendour of
this setting I rested, took off my boots and socks,
soaked my aching feet in the peat-tinted cold water;
cooled my wine, dined on a meal of smoked mackerel
and brown bread and came to the definite conclusion
that if God created anything finer he kept it to himself.

I had brought with me a paperback edition of Bonhoeffer's *Letters and Papers from Prison* and as I lay
there with the sun burning my body and the heat from
the stones and boulders flowing over me in waves, I
read the passage that began this book. It was as if the
door to understanding and realization had opened for
me. I could not have chosen a more realistic setting to
understand the meaning of those words.

Along every mile I had walked — Langcombe Brook,
the Erme, the Avon and across the many brooks and
tributaries that tumbled and bubbled along to feed
them — were scattered the dwelling places, burial
grounds and working areas of the first settlers to
populate Dartmoor. Early Bronze Age, late Bronze
Age, Iron Age, the Celts, they built their communities
around these rivers and streams, which provided water
and food for their stock. They walled them, made
pounds to prevent the animals straying at night; lived
and loved, worked, fought and died. The ground upon
which I walked received their bodies and used them to
invigorate the soil. Willings Walls Warren, Trowlesworthy Warren, with six hut circles and a large pound;

19

Erme Pound, Erme Plains — more evidence of agricultural communities; Huntingdon Warren has a large settlement on both sides of the Avon as it journeys on from here, sweeping beneath Huntingdon Clapper Bridge, under Whitebarrow across Abbot's Way to the reservoir. Zeal Plains, Black Tor, Shipley Tor — almost every foot of the way into South Brent carries monuments to their existence.

At that moment, with the sun burrowing its way into my system, I reached back along its rays to the very source of its power and seemed to establish an affinity with those early moorland dwellers. Through four thousand years I established a rapport, a feeling of awe, of primaeval longing akin to worship. The sun was life itself. How those men must have cherished every second of its daily appearance, prayed to it, prayed for it, cursed its absence through the long winters of its neglect. Every aspect of their lives revolved around it. It brought warmth to ripen their crops, revive their stock, nourish and thaw their frozen bodies into rebirth. For these ancients it was the only comprehensible God. For a brief moment I became one with them, felt as they felt, and the feeling was derived from the same source, the life source — the sun.

I was carried back nearly forty years to boyhood in the Lancashire village of Summerseat where I worked as a weft carrier in a cotton mill. During the only break of the day, lunch, I would escape from the mind-shattering 'clackety-clacking' of five hundred looms into the quiet of the wooded valley by the river Irwell. It was here by the pond which fed its waters into the mill's Lancashire boiler that I became aware of the sun for the first time. I was lying face-down in the grass trying to hold back the seconds ticking away the limits of my freedom. The sun was hot on my back, and growing hotter every minute. It enveloped my whole body, penetrating my being, willing me not to return to the work I hated; but to stay there soaking in its warmth, revelling in its promised escape.

All that afternoon, locked in the dank, dark atmosphere of the weaving shed I could feel that source enticing me, compelling me to leave, to do anything, anywhere, that would grant me the freedom of the open air. Finally I obeyed it, never to return. Since then, whatever work I have been compelled to do, however successful I have been in the doing of it, the sun has always intervened, drawing me like a magnet back to the open, unfettered and alone . . .

. . . I gathered my things together, pulled on my boots and prepared to walk across Huntingdon Warren, and as I travelled I realized I could never again regard these ancient remains in the old way. They were no longer objects left behind by the dead of past centuries, but living reminders of human endeavour, suffering, weakness and courage.

Over to the right, the location of the old Warrener's House stark in its isolation, the most lonely dwelling on the moor, with the Western Walla Brook as its private watering place. I wondered if John Michelmore, the Warrener, was happy here. Did he live alone? If not, how did his wife survive the months without human companionship, with only the occasional winter visitor, out hunting, for company and conversation. Did she accompany her husband as he worked, building his 'burys', stocking them, perhaps holding the poles as he stretched his nets from burrow to burrow. Rising with him in the morning's dark to drive, with their dogs, the rabbits into captivity. Through the long winters, when the snow blanketed these naked slopes, and the wind sliced through their shivering bodies, did they work as one, carrying hay for the rabbits starving in their holes, unable to reach the pathetically inadequate natural source of their diet, buried deep in the frozen snow. Was there no one sufficiently interested in them as 'people' to leave behind for us some insight into their lives?

It was now late afternoon. My eyes ached from the sun's glare, my legs were weary, my body hot and sticky, my brain bursting with the wonder of the day.

Thurber was equally tired as head down, tongue lolling, she loped by my side. We breasted Pupers Hill to see the last lap stretching out before us in sun-bathed beauty. Buckfastleigh Moor and Scorriton Down. For the first time, there were trees. To my right Clarkes Barn Plantation and Scae Wood. On the left Gibby Combe Wood. Walking all day, I had at no time missed trees, but now, seeing their cool green foliage draped around me, I could not conceive a landscape without them. Crossing the river at Chalk Ford, we walked towards Scorriton and the pint I had been dreaming about.

I sat for a long while in the Tradesmans Arms, drinking my beer and gazing out over the moor, letting the events of the day flow over me, filling me with a strange, inexplicable joy. It was as if the physical exertions of the walk had heightened my mental perception giving it clarity and depth. This was not just another ordinary day. This was different. This was a glorious day. Even more, this was *my* day — my day of glory. That was it. Glory.

Vauvenargues wrote of it:

> Glory is now a discredited word and it will be difficult to re-establish it. It has been spoilt by a too close association with fame and ambition. But true glory is a private and discreet virtue and is only fully realized in solitariness.

True glory found in solitariness can still be realised in the peace that is Dartmoor, provided the seeker searches with the innocence and joy of the child or the poet, and is aware, as was John Clare, at the age of five:

> I wanted to find the brink of the world. To look down like looking into a large pit and see into its secrets the same as I believed I could see heaven by looking into the water. So I eagerly wandered on

and rambled along the furze the whole day, till I got out of my knowledge. The very sun seemed to be a new one and shining in a different quarter of the sky still I felt no fear, my wonder-seeking happiness had no room for it.

John Clare never visited Dartmoor yet in one poem, *Song*, he conveyed totally the response the moor evokes in those who love it.

Swamps of wild rush-beds, and sloughs' squashy
  traces,
Grounds of rough fallows with thistle and weed,
Flats and low valleys of kingcups and daisies,
Sweetest of subjects are ye for my reed:
Ye commons left free in the rude rags of nature,
Ye brown heaths bedclothed in furze as ye be,
My wild eye in rapture adores every feature,
Ye are dear as this heart in my bosom to me.

O native endearments! I would not forsake ye,
I would not forsake ye for sweetest of scenes;
For sweetest of gardens that nature could make me,
I would not forsake ye, dear valleys and greens:
Tho' nature ne'er dropt ye a cloud-resting mountain,
Nor waterfalls tumble their music so free;
Had nature denied ye a bush, tree, or fountain,
Ye still had been lov'd as an Eden by me.

And long, my dear valleys, long, long may ye flourish,
Though rush-beds and thistles make most of your
  pride;
May showers never fail the green's daisies to nourish,
Nor suns dry the fountain that rills by its side,
Your skies may be gloomy, and misty your mornings,
Your flat swampy valleys unwholesome may be;
Still, refuse of nature, without her adornings
Ye are dear as this heart in my bosom to me.

II

BUCKLAND BEACON

The honest explorer, rejoicing in Dartmoor's visual splendour, is nevertheless aware that a landscape bearing no human element upon its surface is artificial. Not the manufactured humanity that adds an aura of classical detachment to a landscape by Claude, but that of Millet whose figures grow out of the soil they work, and whose forms and contours are extensions of their landscape, which, without them would be barren and soulless. In the same way, the workers of Dartmoor have left their outline upon its surface for all who have eyes to see.

Such a worker is W. Arthur Clement who lives in Exmouth; his work on Dartmoor will outlast time. He turned an isolated location which for centuries rarely saw a visitor into a place almost of pilgrimage. Now, many journey on the road from Ashburton to Buckland in the Moor and leave their cars on the road verges by Welstor Common and make the easy climb up Buckland Beacon. Their reasons are two-fold. This one thousand three hundred foot landmark rewards the climber with one of the most magnificent views found anywhere. The Dart valley twists and turns its way beneath, through Holne Chase and away to the almost too perfect landscape of the South Hams. On a warm, mist free day the Channel can be seen shimmering in the distance, and northwards are the dominating heights of Rippon, Saddle and Haytor. Late evening is the best time with the setting sun thrusting up blood red tentacles that cling to the granite outcrops, resisting extinction to the last, dying second.

Most visitors however, are not aware of the view that Arthur Clement saw every day. They discover it by accident. It is Arthur's work they have come to see: The Ten Commandments carved into two slabs of granite. The reasons for this extraordinary feat of craftsmanship are best told as Arthur told them to me:

'It was the summer of 1928. Mr Whitley, who lived at Welstor, close by the Beacon, informed me it was his intention to have me carve the Ten Commandments to commemorate the defeat in Parliament of the Revised Prayer Book and to record the dates of the readings of the Bill:

> December 15th 1927
> June 14th 1928

He had selected two granite rocks lying at the base of the Tor, these seeming to him similar in the position they lay, to the two tablets mentioned in the Book of Exodus.

'A colleague and I set to work to dress the stone down to a workable face, which proved quite a task as the granite had become surprisingly tough through long exposure. Upon completion, my companion left me, and with the aid of a Prayer Book I proceeded to mark out all the Commandments. A quotation which was a favourite of Mr Whitley followed the fourth Commandment:

> *But there's a power, which man can wield*
> *When mortal aid is vain,*
> *That eye, that arm, that love to reach,*
> *That listening ear to gain*
> That power is prayer.

'During this operation Mr Whitley paid several visits to the Beacon, usually on horseback, accompanied by several dogs, and it was during one of these visits he decided to call me "Moses". To which I remarked:

"It is rather inappropriate, sir, as Moses carried the tablets of stone down to the children of Israel, and I have no intention of doing that."

'After setting out the Tenth Commandment there was a considerable space left and I suggested he might like the "Eleventh Commandment" in the New Testament from the book of John, Chapter 13 Verse 34, and also the third verse from the hymn *O God Our Help in Ages Past*. He readily agreed and I commenced engraving the letters into the rock.

'Day after day I was on my knees chipping away, as though in an attitude of prayer. I wonder if the originator of the Commandments suffered from aching back or sore knees as I did.

'The work was commenced on July 23rd 1928, and was completed on August 31st, 1928. My place of abode during this work was situated in the woods beneath the Beacon, being more or less a cattle shed, with a hayloft over. My bed was rudely fashioned with wire netting for a mattress and blankets I had brought with me, as the nights were rather cold. Strange as it seems I did not feel lonely. With a candle for illumination I would retire about 9 p.m. and read a bit before settling down. The screeching of owls and barking of foxes kept me awake the first night, but afterwards I was soon asleep. After a good wash in the stream close by, and preparing a very varied breakfast and packing up some food I journeyed once more to the Beacon.

'At last, after several weeks' stay, the task was completed and approved by Mr Whitley. Having survived the elements (which were at times vicious), and "roughing it", it was with mixed feelings that I gathered up my tools to leave the beautiful spot, feeling that I had done a good job, and it was with reluctance that I shaved off my beard before returning to "civilization", having by this time the appearance of a true "Moorman".'

Few people have more right to that title than Arthur Clement. Every time I visit the Beacon now I think of him working away in isolation in this setting. Perhaps walking to church on a Sunday morning down the Tor path towards farm gates, taking the one on the left past Welstor, continuing down the hill to the lane leading to Haytor, and after about a mile, turning left to find the Church of Buckland in the Moor facing him, with its clock without numbers, instead the words 'My dear mother' spelled out around the face. This Church of St Peter was originally built in the twelfth century but only the font, the south wall of the nave and south doorway survive from that period. It was rebuilt and added to in the thirteenth, fifteenth and sixteenth centuries, and finally in the eighteenth century the pulpit and Royal Arms were added. The scattered houses around the village, like the church, are built of grey moorstone and are almost all thatched, giving the parish a timelessness and aura of gentility alien to the surrounding Tors and moorland.

This feeling of unreality is continued by leaving the village through the woods that line the valley of the river Webburn as it flows to join the Dart under Buckland Bridge, at Holne Chase. Here the river Dart travels its tempestuous course over a granite-bouldered bed, making a 'U' turn through a deeply wooded valley, mainly of oaks, and passing under two fifteenth century bridges built in 1413 of local moorstone. Once, these woods echoed to the note of the hunting horn, as this was an area set apart for the hunting of deer, fox and marten, but it was not part of the privileged Royal Forest. This was a setting remembered by writer Charles Kingsley, and above this valley is the greystone village of Holne, where Kingsley was born in 1819, the son of the Curate in charge. Sadly, Kingsley is out of fashion today, but *Westward Ho!* is for me a masterpiece of English historical fiction and many's the time I have sailed out of Barnstaple Bay with Salvation Yeo, Will Cary and Amyas Leigh to battle at Margarita, or to take the *Great Galleon*. Often I have wept at blind Amyas, clasping the savage Indian girl Ayacanora to his heart, crying: 'What God has joined together man cannot put asunder', a sentiment not universally

accepted today and more likely to provoke derision.
Kingsley believed it. He was a happily married man
until his early death at the age of fifty-five and this was
his intent:

*I would sing about the blossoms, the sunshine and the
  sky,
And the tiny wife I mean to have in such a cosy nest;
And if someone came and shot me dead, why then I
  should but die
With my tiny life and tiny song just ended at their best.*

Kingsley was a remarkable man who became Canon
of Westminster and Professor of Modern History at
Cambridge. He was concerned about social injustice
and wrote pamphlets, including *Politics for the People*,
and his children's story, *The Waterbabies*, to arouse
public concern for the poor. His poetry is equally neglected, although even in verse he managed to champion
the underdog. In this case the maligned North East
wind:

*Welcome, wild North-Easter!
Shame it is to see
Odes to every zephyr;
Ne'er a verse to thee.*

The visual aspect of Holne has altered little since
Kingsley's day. It is still a joy to walk around, visit the
church with its memorial windows bearing Kingsley's
portrait and his motto 'Be Strong'. Wander in the
churchyard where William Crossing deciphered the
inscription on the weathered gravestone of Edward
Collins:

*Here lies poor old Ned,
On his last mattress bed,
During his life he was honest and free;
He knew well the Chace
But has now run his race
And his name was Collins d'ye fee.*

Ned died in 1780 and was for many years landlord of the Church House Inn where I have sunk many a pleasant pint on my journeys from Tavistock to Buckfastleigh.

One thing I have never witnessed in Holne is the Ram Roasting ceremony which used to take place on Green Down every Midsummer Day, for like so many of the customs and pastimes of the working community of Dartmoor, this one has been allowed to lapse.

A walk of less than five miles from Holne, crossing Kings Wood, Wallaford Down, leads to Dean Wood. Through the wood runs Dean-Bourn (now spelt 'Burn'), 'a rude river', often visited and thus described by poet Robert Herrick who lived a short step away at Dean Prior. He came here as Vicar, being offered the living in 1629, and stayed for sixteen years until being rejected as a Royalist by Cromwell. After the Restoration he returned in 1662 and remained until his death in 1674.

Herrick was born a Cockney in London's Cheapside on August 24th, 1591. It is believed he went to school at Westminster, evidence of this being derived from lines in his poem, *Golden Cheapside*:

> *Never again shall I with finny oar*
> *Put from or draw unto the faithful shore;*
> *And landing here, or safely landing there,*
> *Make way to my beloved Westminster,*
> *or to the Golden Cheapside where the couch*
> *of Julia Herrick gave me my birth.*

At sixteen he left school and became apprenticed to his Uncle William Herrick, a goldsmith. Splendid gold and silver work was produced during the seventeenth century in England and Herrick must have taken an artistic and creative delight in the craft, even if he found his situation uncongenial. But it was his employment after working hours in his beloved Cheapside that helped to formulate his future creative direction.

James I was on the throne, Shakespeare in the final

flood of dramatic creation. *Anthony and Cleopatra* and *King Lear* were in production. Ben Johnson was at the height of his fame and popularity and Herrick would have thrilled to performances of *Volpone*, *The Alchemist* and *The Silent Woman*. He would have known the works of Dekker and Heywood and the widening of his horizons brought on a restlessness and discontent which forced him to free himself from his uncle's apprenticeship and become a student at Cambridge. He took his B.A. in 1616-17 and M.A. in 1620.

It is not known how Herrick spent the eight years after he left Cambridge, although it is certain his friendship with Ben Johnson developed at this time. They met nightly with other poets after an afternoon theatre performance, quaffing bumpers of sack and canary; roistering and talking into the early hours. They drank in the Mermaid, the Mitre and Windmill taverns, later transferring their allegiance to the Dog and Triple Tun.

From the calm of his pastoral hermitage at Dean Prior, Herrick wrote lovingly of Johnson and those Cheapside days:

> *Ah Ben*
> *Say how or when,*
> *Shall we, thy guests,*
> *Meet at those lyric feasts*
> *Made at the Sun,*
> *The Dog, the Triple Tun?*
>
> *When we such clusters had*
> *As made us nobly wild, not mad;*
> *And yet each verse of thine*
> *Outdid the meat, outdid the frolic wine.*

The Dean Prior of Herrick's day was described as 'a place approached by quiet hamlets and pleasant meadows with here and there a glimpse of distant hills, with the church and vicarage set amid trees in a deep narrow valley.'

Yesterday's quiet hamlets are, alas, no more. The A38 dual carriageway runs alongside the church and vicarage today polluting the air with smells and noise, destroying the quiet of the vicarage garden where, surrounded by spring's offering of wild daffodils, gleaming golden in the dawn, Herrick wrote one of his best-loved poems:

> *Faire Daffodils, we weep to see*
> *You haste away so soone;*
> *As yet the early-rising Sun*
> *Has not attained his Noone.*

And this same garden setting inspired another poem heralding spring's awakening:

> *TO VIOLETS*
> *Welcome maids of honour,*
> *You do bring*
> *In the spring*
> *And wait upon her.*

Herrick's life at Dean Prior was a perpetual love-hate relationship between his awareness of the blessings derived from his rural existence:

> *Lord, thou hast given me a cell*
> *Wherein to dwell;*
> *A little house whose humble roof*
> *Is weather-proof;*
> *Under the sparres of which I lie*
> *Both soft and drie . . .*

. . . and regret at his enforced isolation and separation from London and his friends:

> *More discontents I never had*
> *Since I was born, than here;*
> *Where I have been and still am sad*
> *In this dull Devonshire . . .*

His regrets were always less powerful than his love for his surroundings and his knowledge that here was the source of creative inspiration that earned him his title, 'England's sweetest lyric Poet'.

Take a copy of *Hesperides* with you when you visit Dean Prior. Open your eyes to the spell of this most beautiful of countrysides; and your hearts to the lyrical magic of Herrick's verse.

You will not find Herrick's grave in the churchyard, nor that of his faithful housekeeper-companion Prudence Baldwin, for their resting places are unmarked.

Herrick requires no gravestone epitaph. *Hesperides* contains sufficient for the reader to choose his or her own tribute. My choice would undoubtedly be that verse transposed from the lines of a character in Dekker's delightful comedy, *The Shoemaker's Holiday:*

TO BE MERRY
Let's now take our time,
While we're in our prime,
And old, old age is afar off;
For the evil, evil days
Will come on apace
Before we can be aware of.

III

FERNWORTHY RESERVOIR

'Hoink-hoink-hoink, come arn, come arn, hoink-hoink, come arn. . . .'

That was how I first met Sidney Potter, the resident Warden at Fernworthy reservoir, standing thigh deep in the water, arms out-stretched, talking down a flight of Canadian Geese. Each time the flight's circle grew smaller and smaller, lower and lower, until they splashed down on the water and, completely unafraid, sailed up to take bread from his hand.

'Took me a long time', he said, 'but they know me now, visit me morning and evening. They be started nesting at the north end. Perhaps we might persuade them to breed here.'

Fernworthy Reservoir was opened on 22nd June, 1942. It was built as a water catchment to facilitate the requirements of the sources supplying the areas of Bovey Tracey, Newton Abbot and Torquay. Its water is obtained by damming the upper valley of the South Teign river. It is the last all-granite dam built on the moor. I find it the most pleasant — both in construction and setting within the moorland scene and, of course, it has Sidney Potter.

'I joined the Water Authority in 1926, so you might say I spent fifty years of my life with water. It's the most wonderful job any man could have here at Fernworthy. I love the freedom, you see, the open air, the moorland. It's never the same, you see, never the same. Always something new, always something going on. It's a very busy life and a very full life. Seventy-six acres my area covers. I walk part of it every day.

Hundreds of miles I walk in a year. Twenty-six years I've spent here and I'll spend another twenty-six if they let me.

'It's perfect here for a man who loves solitude and the countryside. I've Fernworthy forest to walk through. It's like having a private wood. There are cairns and hut circles in the forest, stretching back thousands of years, including the famous Fernworthy circle, almost a true circle that is, with twenty-seven standing stones nearly fifty feet in diameter. Over there on Shovel Down they've two perfect stone rows — one is six hundred feet long — and two standing stones, Longstone and Three Boys.

'If I glance up when I'm out walking there's Thornworthy Tor overseeing the dam, making sure everything is in order.

'On the north west bank you can see the remains of Fernworthy farm, a real old Dartmoor farm that was built in 1590 on the site of an even older farm. Built of solid granite taken from these outcrops. They shouldn't 've done that. It upset the elves who live inside the hill. They crept down to the farm one night and stole away the farmer's new born son as punishment for stealing their stone. At least, that's what they do say about Fernworthy farm. It was demolished when they built the reservoir. They had to flood the old trackway and the clapper bridge as well. Every time we have a long, hot spell the bridge is exposed. People come from all over to see it.

'They come for the fishing as well. It's like greeting old friends when the anglers arrive. Never have time to be lonely, you see. I have my avenue. Potter's Avenue they call it now. It used to be Elliot road. I started planting it when I first arrived, using my spare time, and out of my own pocket. Now it's like a small wood covering the slope from the dam to the water. All rhododendron. You should see them in bloom. Wonderful sight. Wonderful.

'It's the water I really love. I'm a religious man. Do a lot of preaching around the moor — Chagford, Ashburton, Buckfastleigh. I'm known for that. I find the water like the Bible. Always something to turn to, to seek solace in, to uplift a sad soul, to clear the mind of confusion. I love walking by running water, listening to the tunes it's playing. Sometimes it will speak to me, quietly, gently. Other times it shouts ordering me: ''Don't despair, live on, live on.'' I'm never happier than by water.

'I wanted to leave something behind to explain what all this has meant to me. I decided to carve a text on the ''Heath Stone'' on Chagford Common. I chose a text from St John's Gospel:

Jesus said, I am the way, the truth, and the light.

'I'm afraid that's all I managed to carve. I was stopped doing any more. There should've been more lines but I wasn't allowed to finish them. It seems it was an offence against the Dartmoor preservation and conservation laws.

'Seems funny that — the word of our Lord an offence against conservation. I've spent my life believing that all this belonged to him.'

IV

STICKLEPATH

The village of Sticklepath lies at the foot of Cawsand Hill. At least it does if the walker is using the name given on the Ordnance Survey map of the area. Most of the locals in the village however, are adamant that the name should still be what it once was, 'Cosdon' or 'Cosson Hill'.

William Crossing, the author of *Guide to Dartmoor*, never believed there was any basis for its being called Cawsand. There is something distinctly 'prissy' about the name Cawsand, whereas Cosdon sounds as solid and durable as the hill itself, which spreads over most of South Tawton Common, rising to a height of 1,799 feet. It's a great pity that travellers between Exeter and Cornwall barely give Sticklepath a second glance, regarding it mainly as a village where frustrating traffic hold-ups occur throughout the summer.

Spend a day in Sticklepath. You will enjoy it and at the same time gain in experience and understanding of the true industrial, agricultural and spiritual life of a once important Devon village. A life that revolved around the waters of the River Taw which provided all the power for the village industries. The Taw flows behind the village between Dartmoor and the main A30. Half a mile above the road bridge the river is dammed and a leat runs from it, through the village, to re-join the Taw at a point where it passes under the road.

At one time Sticklepath was known as the village of waterwheels, for it had seven in operation providing the power for corn mills, a woollen mill and a candle factory. In 1804 William Finch set up business in the village as an iron founder, taking over the woollen mill for this purpose, and the corn mill was absorbed by the foundry in 1835 and turned into a grinding house. The foundry operated in this manner until the end of the first world war when William Finch's three sons — Albany, James and Thomas — formed a partnership, buying the property outright and expanding the business.

They advertised as Agricultural and Edge Tool and Shovel Manufacturers and Importer Merchants and Factors. I have in my possession one of their original catalogues giving a list of their wares and trading facilities, with drawings of cross and side handle hay knives, scythe snaths, Cornish shovels, Devon shovels, Cornish square shovels, West Cornwall round pattern shovels, the improved patent poultry coop and the impassable mole trap. These were just a few examples of tools produced for the requirements of china clay workers, Dartmoor and Cornish miners and agricultural workers. The firm also acted as wheelwrights, made carts and barrows, gates and hurdles and even supplied ready-cut boat knees to boatyards. The handles for all the tools were made and fitted at the foundry.

Three waterwheels powered the foundry, the largest driving two trip-hammers and power shears in the forge. The second drove a fan which produced currents of air through underground ducts to the hearths and furnaces. The third was the power source for a large sanstone grinding wheel, which provided the 'edge' to all the cutting tools leaving the foundry, the edge of the stone being bevelled to make it easier to grind shaped blades.

For one hundred and forty years the Finch foundry made a substantial contribution to the economic and social life of Sticklepath, providing work for twenty men and the wheelwrights' and blacksmiths' shops became an amenity — a meeting place for local craftsmen.

The flow of mass produced tools from the Industrial

North and Midlands and the increasing use of machinery on farms caused the gradual decline of the foundry, and when the south wall collapsed in 1960 a whole way of life collapsed with it.

It was the idea of Richard Baron, a descendant of the Finch family, to try and rescue the derelict foundry from total extinction and turn it into a Museum of Rural Industry, but sadly he died before the completion of his project. He would be a proud man if he could see the results of his enterprise today.

Whenever I visit the foundry I remember standing with Bob Baron, listening as he explained with great enthusiasm the plans for the Museum and how he hoped it would become a centre for all who cherished the preservation of ancient crafts and skills. As we talked, the rain poured through a gaping hole in the roof and the wind whistled around us from the shambles of collapsed walls and timbers.

The film we made that day, I hope, will be a permanent reminder of the dedication and sheer hard graft that turned this chaos into one of the country's most fascinating and entertaining museums.

On a more recent visit, I watched a coach party from Scotland gaze spellbound as Bob set the great wheel in motion, demonstrating the working of the trip hammer and using the shears to slice through a square of iron, like scissors cutting paper. Outside, under the waterwheel, oblivious to the water dripping on them from the wood launder, a bluff Yorkshire engineer and a deep South cotton-belt American argued the merits of gearing on other waterwheels of their acquaintance.

The Finch foundry is once again injecting life into the community of Sticklepath and all who helped in this venture can feel justly proud of their efforts.

Bob Baron is devoted to the Finch foundry and to every facet of life that was part of his boyhood. Sitting with him amidst the ever-growing confusion of papers, charts, maps and books that make up what he laughingly describes as his 'office', he talks lovingly of playing truant from school so that he could walk in the peace and solitude of the moor. Sometimes he would spend the night sleeping rough on the sites where once the masons cut and shaped the granite into blocks where it lay in clitters on the hillside, drinking themselves into oblivion with cider at night in order to forget the cold that otherwise would have kept them awake. Often Bob would travel further, to spend the day at the peatworks with the turf cutters.

A talented engineer, although not by profession, he has built a waterwheel on the side of his house and uses it to provide all his heating requirements. On the last occasion we met for a pint across the road from his home, at the Taw River Inn — another good reason for visiting Sticklepath — a very angry Bob had just returned from visiting an old lady living alone near Meldon, frightened out of her wits by an official communication from a bureaucrat.

We talked of her and others like her, the 'expendable' dwellers on present day Dartmoor. That section of the community who, although most entitled to it, have practically no voice in the future of Dartmoor. Those pioneers and their descendants who opened up the moor for us all. Trod its paths and tracks with their ill-clad feet; walked it, built its dwellings, pubs and churches; laid its roads, nursed its stock, quarried its granite, utilised its mineral wealth. The only community to reap from the moor that which they had personally sown. Treading in their footsteps have come the 'experts', tramping the moor, measuring, tabulating, recording, arguing and contradicting. Each concerned with the conservation of 'things'. No place anywhere in their calculations for the conservation of 'people'. No research fellowships for discovering ways of preserving the only village carpenter, blacksmith, shepherd or labourer.

The moormen's humble homes have been converted for their use. The simple one up and down shepherd's cottage becomes a luxury dwelling for the custodian of 'things'. A miner's cottage rented to a working family in 1960 for seven shillings and twopence a week is now part of an £18,000 conversion. Farm houses which once lived through the joys and sorrows of generations of the same family, are retreats for London-based executives, whilst other such farms have remained derelict for years and the cottages around them.

We also discussed the warmth and friendliness of the people of Sticklepath towards visitors, which is hardly surprising, for it has for centuries been called the 'Friendly Village'. The reason for this can be traced to the Finch foundry, for here, almost on the bank of the Taw, watched over by Cosdon Beacon, is the charming and peaceful old Quaker burial ground. A tombstone bears the inscription: 'Take heed to entertain strangers', taken from Hebrews 13, Verse 2, which in its original form reads: 'Be not forgetful to entertain strangers for thereby some have entertained Angels unawares.'

During the reign of Charles II, over two hundred villagers, almost the entire population, were Quakers. It is thought they came to Sticklepath to avoid the severe persecution they suffered throughout the rest of the country. Three parishes met here: South Tawton, Belstone and Sampford Courtney. Taking advantage of the laws of that time the Quakers could easily slip from parish to parish, thus avoiding harassment. The Quaker community dwindled away towards the end of the eighteenth century. Today the village is remembered more for its association with John Wesley.

On Thursday, 22nd September 1743, Wesley travelled from Launceston to Exeter and recorded of that day: 'As we were riding through a village called Sticklepath one stopped me and asked abruptly: "Is not they name John Welsey?" Immediately two or three more came up and told me I must stop there. I did so and before we had spoken many words, our souls took acquaintance with each other. I find they were called "Quakers", but that hurt me not, seeing the Love of God was in their hearts.'

Wesley became fond of Sticklepath and on his journeys between Exeter and Cornwall often preached there to an appreciative audience, for writing again in 1743 he states: 'A storm of hail and rain began while I was preaching but the congregation did not move.'

He preached in an 'open place', now assumed to be from a rock on the Mount, a hill on the west end of the village marked by a flagpole kept in immaculately white condition all the year round. From here he could look across to Cleave Mill on the river bank where serge cloth for the troops of the Nizam of Hyderabad was manufactured in the 1800s. The mill stands sad and deserted today, needing urgent restoration.

Behind the mill across the Taw, Skaigh Wood clings to the final slope of Cosdon and the walk from the foundry along the river bank past the weir to the first bridge is one of the joys Sticklepath owes to Bob Baron. Almost single-handed he cut the path that has now become a regular route for ramblers and tourists and the means by which I left the village and made my way up to Belstone Cleave.

The weeks of drought and early warmth had given way to heavy rain and as I walked the Cleave, the Taw gently murmured its way alongside, journeying to join the Torridge and together flow over the sandbar at Appledore. The foliage that enveloped me was fresh from new birth with late buds exploding into leafy starbursts. Somewhere ahead a cuckoo hurled defiance at all who challenged its aggressive way of life, confident in the knowledge that the villain must at all times be championed and protected — the only crime is to be a victim.

I left the Cleave at Ford, near where the Junior Leaders' Regiment have built a wooden foot bridge, and began the ascent of Cosdon. A strong westerly following wind blew me up the hill with my face into the sun. Cosdon can be climbed from almost any direction, for the heather pile provides a thick ground cover that is not unpleasant for walking. Here and there sheep tracks, about a foot wide, and open to the grass, can be followed to the summit. I have often wondered about these tracks. Do the sheep create them entirely by trampling down the plants or do they assist the process by urination . . . Wherever I looked the formation of new tracks could be distinguished by a faint brown scar etched into the ground as if by acid. Upon inspection, the heather stems and leaves gave no indication of having been crushed or broken. I paused on the track leading to Small Brook, alongside the Ivy Tor water, now dry and sunbaked, and I rested, looking back to Belstone one of my favourite villages on the moor. Bathed in bright sunlight, it shone and sparkled, the church tower of St Mary silhouetted against a backcloth of tall sycamores forming a screen for the east side of the churchyard.

Nearly all the houses surrounding the village are **screened and protected by tall trees and multi-coloured flowering shrubs.** No tawdry products of modern property developers pollute the skyline and the granite-built farms and village cottages rise up naturally out of the soil that gave them birth. The old Zion chapel built in 1841, now converted to a village post office; the **village green and old stocks,** provide an atmosphere of permanency and durability I find invigorating.

Behind the village, Belstone Tor dominates the skyline. Clinging tenaciously to its slope, 'Irishman's Wall' disappears over the summit down the far side. Built by Irish labourers imported to enclose common land against the wishes of the people, who rose up in anger to frustrate the undertaking, it stands as a historical reminder of the liberties taken by those with money and power over the lives of the less fortunate.

I continued to the summit, making for the stone cairn that gives the hill its name, Cosdon Beacon, passing the remains of two kistvaens, stone slab memorials vandalised for wall building purposes. The previous day's rain had cleaned the atmosphere leaving it clear and sharp. The surrounding countryside unsullied· by smog or haze, slashed by sunlight, unscarred by motorways — for the A30 was hidden by field banks — unfolded away to the north coast, as in those wondrous landscapes by Pieter Breughel. Acre

upon acre of rich farmland, ploughed fields, russet
brown and ochre, lime-splashed and planted, grazing
meadows dotted with slow moving black and white
contented cattle, the lush green as yet unburned by
summer's sun. The whole criss-crossed by banks and
hedgerows holding the landscape together as though
caught in the cod end of a trawl. In the far distance the
sea flashed back the sun's rays, bouncing the reflections off the purple-shadowed undulations that were
the hills of Exmoor.

> *And in the meadows and the lower grounds*
> *Was all the sweetness of a common dawn.*

Turning slowly westward the industrially phallic
pretence on Kit Hill leads the eye to Bodmin Moor.
South-west and the aspect changes, the fertile landscape gives way to Dartmoor, bare and treeless save
for the solitary blackthorn defying nature clinging
stubbornly to the windswept hillside. The hills roll
persistently away to the southern skyline. In the light
of a still-climbing sun, the shadows soften the contours,
making them inviting to the unwary. Yes Tor, High
Willhayes, Great Link Tors, Kitty Tor and on to Rattlebrook Hill. Due south, Fur Tor, Rough Tor, Hanging-
stone Hill and Hound Tor and in the far distance the
twin summits of Hay Tor.

Every hilltop seemed to be crowned by a bright red
flag displayed against the blue of the sky by a westerly
wind. The occasional rumbling of guns adding empha-
sis to the warning they proclaimed. Almost the whole
area of visible Tors form an army training area.

Eastwards the bleak moorland changes again, becoming softer, more inviting. Woods, copses, meadows
and streams break up the landscape. The Forest of
Fernworthy sprawls across Chagford Common, Thornworthy and Shovel Down. The windows of Chagford
pick up the sunlight, flash it back skywards like an
enormous torch. The modest summits of Meldon Hill
and Nottadown Common converge into one, leaving the

traveller a slender hole to crawl through.

The Teign, aping one of its own fresh-hooked sea trout, twists and turns, leaps and runs, finally disappearing into the leafy security of Whiddon Wood.

I am alone. I am king. I have all this. Who has more? Solitude and peace and a landscape of bewildering complexity and beauty — without a single human being to threaten my inheritance. Life is good. Somewhere down there the world is going about its awful occasions. Here only a solitary skylark giving a command performance to an audience of one.

This moment will remain forever, retained in the filing cabinet of memory, and be used again and again as an antidote against the ugliness and chaos of modern existence.

It is time to move on, downwards, crossing Cheriton Combe, passing between South Tawton and Throwleigh Commons. The slope of Cosdon that runs out into South Tawton Common and away to West Week has always intrigued me. It is festooned with walls, hanging on the hillsides like delicate crochet work. Nowhere else on Dartmoor do walls so forcibly thrust themselves upon the notice of the passer-by, as if apologizing for the pointlessness of their existence. Any gates which might have divided field from field have long since gone, and stock wander where they will. Gaping holes appear where the walls have succumbed to the movement of the earth beneath, in the winter's frost, and where cattle rubbed their itching backsides for relief. All that skill and hard labour for such little purpose.

> *Before I built a wall I'd ask to know*
> *What I was walling in or walling out,*
> *And to whom I was like to give offence.*
> *Something there is that doesn't love a wall,*
> *That wants it down.*
>
> Robert Frost

Heading towards Throwleigh I cross the Blakaton Brook at the ford above the weir and pass between

Moor Farm and Clannaborough. Clannaborough Farm, an early mediaeval construction examples of which still remain behind the present farmhouse, is the home of the Endacott family. Some years ago I visited them to talk with Alan, one of the teenage sons, who — despite his youth — had announced the opening of his one-man museum.

His first encouragement came whilst walking the moor and finding a civil war cannon ball. His museum, housed in one of his father's barns alongside the farmhouse, grew to consist of three separate sections. He collected a unique display of farm implements, equipment and machinery. Friends, neighbours, indeed anybody who may have had something of interest or value, were persuaded by Alan to part with it for his museum. Among many objects, he had a fine collection of minerals, both of this country and elsewhere in the world, so it is not surprising to find him today, grown to manhood, working as a chemist for English China Clay.

His younger brother was pleased to conduct me around, explaining the exhibits and it seems that the Endacotts have another collector and future museum curator in the family.

The museum is open to the public, but it is essential to make a telephone call to arrange an appointment. Clannaborough is a working farm and visitors have to take a second place. But if you make an appointment they will be happy to welcome you.

I left Clannaborough through the village of Throwleigh and made my way towards Gidleigh, picking up the public footpath near Langston to Ash, using the road to the cattle grid and public footpaths once more through Moortown to bring me out close to the castle and church. On almost every occasion when something is written about Dartmoor, a plan for restoration or rebuilding of Gidleigh Castle is mentioned, yet it stands today sad and forlorn, the remains of what must have been a proud thirteenth century fortified manor house, now derelict in a condition too dangerous for visitors.

The Church of the Holy Trinity remains as beautiful as ever, built quite simply of moorland granite, not quarried but taken from the surface during the fifteenth century. It spreads an aura of peace to all who steal time out of life to reap the benefit. I had visited it a few weeks before on a warm spring evening. Inside, the church had been freshly decorated with spring flowers; daffodils and primroses were hanging from the piers, in and around the font and decorating the altar. The scent was overwhelming. Outside, the sound of the gentle running stream crossing the churchyard joined with the clamour of rooks in the wooded glens, and the streams rushing down rock and boulder strewn hillsides, to provide a moment of pure joy. Nothing moved; no voice broke the silence, no dog barked, no cars, not even the sound of a farm tractor disturbed the tranquility of the setting.

All my senses fused, uniting in appreciation of the mood and scene, calmed by the absoluteness of the stillness. Even my skin responded to the caress of the warm spring breeze rustling the elms and moving the daffodils to bow their respects. It was as if the whole world had taken a deep breath and then retained it, fearing the noise of expulsion would break the spell. The release when it came resounded around the church-yard in a banshee wail, disturbing the rooks and identifying itself as the frustrated bellowing of a cow unable to join its comrades in an adjoining field.

Reluctantly woken from my reverie, I prepared for my journey home.

V

CHAGFORD

At home I have a very beautiful porcelain group depicting an old Dartmoor farmer complete with stick, standing beneath an oak talking about the moor to a somewhat taller man who is clutching a microphone, with a large Labrador dog by his side. That man is me. Peering from behind a tree listening intently to the conversation are three sheep.

The group arrived at my cottage as a gift from a very talented artist/potter living in South Molton — Margerie Coning. She modelled it after she had seen the farmer being interviewed on film, and enjoyed him so much she thought I might like something to remember him by. I cherish it for two reasons. Firstly, for the thought and artistry. Secondly, for the fond memories I retain for that wonderful character I was with. His name was Wallace Perryman and I met him some years ago as he sat in the bar of the Ring O' Bells in Chagford, battered hat on head, laying down the law over some recent breach of Dartmoor etiquette.

Wallace Perryman lived at Yeo Farm. Yeo, an example of a typical Dartmoor farmhouse known to hundreds of tourists jammed in the narrow winding lanes, dating back to Saxon times, on the route to Kes Tor. Few, if any, of these travellers, however, waiting with that intensity of impatience characteristic of people enjoying themselves, are aware of the historical significance of the farm.

Yeo Farm was almost certainly the first farm in Britain to have electric power by water wheel and possibly the first private dwelling. The power system was originated by Wallace's grandfather, John, carried on by his father, William, and finally modified and extended by Wallace himself. The power source is the river Teign, running along a mill leat cut by John and later widened by Wallace and carried to the wheel by a wood launder.

The original all-wood wheel was fitted in 1840 but replaced by a metal and wood wheel twenty years later. The electric supply was 'switched on' in January 1893 and has continued functioning to the present day, with only the addition of an electric motor, providing the light for the farmhouse and out-buildings and power for all the machinery. It was adapted by belts and pulleys to drive two large circular saws, one of which is used in conjunction with a four speed rack bench and provides the facilities of a small saw mill. The original driving link was by cog segments around the outside of the wheel, these picking up a drive shaft. This has now been replaced by a chain drive. The strength and power generated by this wheel is illustrated by the knowledge that on two occasions, using three hundred yards of metal hawser across fields, the forward and reverse gear system successfully hauled a tractor from a bog, and winched a heavy lorry which had been spreading lime from the same situation.

For many years the farm operated as a corn mill with two grinding stones, alas no longer working but still in place, a chaff cutter, a winnowing machine for separating corn from the chaff, and a threshing machine, all driven by a straight drive shaft from the wheel and operated by a triple link sprocket with wooden cogs.

The wheel also powered a turnip crusher and Wallace introduced an underground shaft in a pipe, which went across the farmyard to the once very busy blacksmith's shop in order to blow air for the forge. This was worked by the wheel, as was the pump for the domestic water in the farm kitchen. It drove the cream separator, butter churn, washing machine and — believe it or not — a boot-cleaning machine. Another facility operated by the water wheel was a bone-crusher, providing bone meal for fertilizer.

There is also a wood lathe, put to good use by Edgar Loram, husband of Wallace's daughter Frances, and if you should visit the delightful Dartmoor village of North Bovey and call in for a drink at the Ring O' Bells, the skittles they use were made at Yeo Farm by Edgar using the lathe.

The superb skill and craftsmanship that went towards the construction of the water wheel is still apparent today. As it rotates it shows no sign of wear and runs as straight and true as the day it was installed. Edgar Loram greases the bearings twice a week, and when I last visited he had been using the circular saw to cut and fit new boards for the wheel.

The ingenuity of Wallace Perryman in adapting the wheel to so many different usages is still visible in the multiplicity of belts and pulleys, which had to be changed every time a different machine was used. Every machine ran at a different speed and the adaption of gear ratio was nothing less than a work of pure genius.

This adaptability was a characteristic of all old 'moormen' and in Wallace's case was a family inheritance. He often spoke to me of his grandfather John:

'We had no police force in Chagford y'see, so my grandfather was sworn in as a parish constable in the early 1800's. If there was any trouble, like a fight or poaching, and he made an arrest, he would take the prisoner to the ''Shambles'' in the square near the butcher's shop and lock 'em up in the prison.. There were eight of these parish constables and they all had a key to the ''lock-up''. Inside there was a bunk with a roll of blankets and two leather pillows.

'Then he'd have to tell the chairman of Moretonhampstead Board of Magistrates, the Reverend William Hames up at the rectory, of the arrest and would be instructed to present the prisoner at Moretonhampstead next morning for sentence. He didn't mind that so much, but if the prisoner was sent to prison it meant him having to walk all the way to Exeter, hand over the prisoner, have a drink and a meal at an inn, and then walk the eighteen miles back to Chagford. Thirty-six miles in one day — and he did this often. I've heard him say he had some rough old customers to deal with and always travelled with two loaded pistols, two sets of handcuffs, large and small, and his staff. The staff was three feet long with five inches of lead in one end and a loop at the other. If any prisoner gave him trouble he thought nothing of giving him a crack over the head and then handcuffing him.

'There was a man called George Clampitt, a boot and shoe maker in Chagford. He was always called ''Cuddy''. He was the *Crowner's* messenger. Whenever a sudden death or suicide took place in the parish, Cuddy would be told. He would change into his uniform and set off on foot to Black Torrington, twenty-five miles away, stopping at Okehampton for a drink and a meal in the George Inn in West Street. At Black Torrington he would receive his orders from the Crowner, who lived there, and be told the date and time of the Crowning and be instructed to book the upstairs room here in the Ring O' Bells.

'Once Cuddy had his instructions he would cross the road to the Torridge Inn, have a meal and then set off back to Okehampton, with further liquid refreshment at the George, reaching there at midnight. He would arrive at Chagford some three hours later.

'At the Crowning would be a twelve man jury and if the death was determined as a suicide the date of burial would be fixed by the Crowner. At that time no suicides were allowed burial in consecrated ground, so the Crowner would ask Cuddy what crossroads were available for burial. Cuddy would then read out the last place of such a burial and what was left available would be agreed upon. Then two gravediggers would dig the grave at night, the bearers would carry the coffin by candlelight and commit it to the ground. No burial service was allowed. The last act of Cuddy was to wait and see the grave covered and returfed.'

Chagford was a fine place to live then. Four fairs a

year held the last Thursday in March, the first Thursday in May, September and October. The square would be full of sheep pens and all the farmers from off the moor made a day of it.

Over two hundred and fifty people were employed here by Mr John Berry of Chagford in the woollen trade. There was the higher factory and lower factory, known as the tucking mill, and the weaving and combing mill. Today it's the Moorlands Hotel.

'Of course tis all different now. Not like it was, not much work here, less you go to Exeter. Mostly retired people come to live here now. Lots of visitors in the summer, that's about it. Nothing stays the same for ever does it?'

Nothing stays the same for ever — not even men of the character of Wallace Perryman, more's the pity. But Chagford is a much better place because he spent eighty-eight years there, and although Wallace is dead, the Perryman family live on at Yeo Farm. Frances, his daughter, is well known wherever horse lovers congregate in the south west. Edgar Loram, her husband, is from the same mould as Wallace. The Lorams of Chagford are known all over Dartmoor and stories of their activities have entered into Dartmoor legend. Edgar Loram was one of a family of seventeen; at the age of twelve he was driving two horses along the steeply sloping woodland of the Teign valley above Fingle Gorge, dragging pine logs from there to Calstock, where they were made into baskets for the strawberry trade.

Edgar has taken over the responsibility of the water wheel and the farm. I'm relieved to know they're in such good hands.

VI

AT THE PEAT WORKS

On a very cold day in November 1964, I was enjoying a quiet pint in the large bar of the Highwayman Inn at Sourton. The Inn stands on the main Tavistock-Okehampton A386 road fringing Dartmoor. The pub is known to tourists from all over Britain for its eye-catching exuberance due to the exterior architecture, and the enterprise and character of its owner, Buster Jones.

Outside, driving wind whipped sleet against the window panes, obscuring the view of Sourton Tors which wore dark brooding clouds on its head like a winter bonnet. Inside was snug and warm, with an enormous log fire blazing, reflecting in its flames the many brass ornaments and domestic utensils hanging from the beams. Above me I noticed a new addition to the collection. A large turf-cutting knife. I asked Buster where it came from.

'That peat cutter? Why, that came from old Walter! Have you never met Walter Alford? You must — he's the last man alive to work at the peat works at the back of Rattlebrook. Come on across the road. I'll introduce you. He lives with his son at the farm.'

Walter was in the sitting room having his hair trimmed by his daughter-in-law. As she snipped away and the grey hairs collected in tiny nests on the towel round his neck, he told me of his life. He was eighty-four, but his memory was still sharp and clear.

'Well, there warn't really any other job to go to, it had to be the peat works. Times was very bad all round, men with families were all out of work around Dartmoor, so I was lucky to be working — a young man and single. There were six of us used to set off every morning from Bridestowe to climb the track to the peat works between Amicombe Hill and Great Links Tor, about six miles it was and all up hill. I remember that bit. Handsome in the summer, with the sun climbing above Amicombe, but bitter in the winter with the rain driving straight in to your face. We'd arrive at the works soaked and work all day in that state. There were buildings to work in, but most of the work was outside, with not so much as a tree for shelter. Sometimes, of course, we wouldn't be wanted for work and would be laid off for seven or eight weeks at a time, and then we'd go back for three or four months. It was always like that.

'We used to cut the peat in "journeys" — that was a row of twenty paces, three turves wide. We'd cut it with a "turveyor". It had a prong on top of the blade so's we could pick up the cut turf without trouble. We'd cut between four feet and six feet depths of turf about eighteen inches long, and then use a "slitting knife" to face them off clean. If there were plenty of peat dried and waiting for transport we would be paid a flat rate of seventeen shillings a week, but if they had a lot of orders we would go on piece work at two shillings a journey. We cut some turves on they days I can tell you. We'd leave them laying where we'd cut them and come back later and stock them up in threes. Drying them out was the problem. It was damp all the time up there. Most of the time working in rain or mist and the peat would never dry out proper. They tried pressing out the water but it crushed the peat as well. Then they built charcoal ovens. It was working on one of they that I lost a finger. Had it crushed. They warn't much use really.

'It was hard work and long hours, especially with the walking over twelve miles a day. 'Course the railway track made a difference. I don't remember an engine like some say. Only horses to pull the trucks up from Bridestowe and around the sidings at the works. Sometimes we would ride back in the trucks using long poles wedged against the wheels as a brake. If the pole snapped you hit the Bridestowe siding a hell of a wallop. Oh, it was a tough life, but like I said, there wasn't no other so you did it.'

When I said farewell to Walter the weather had changed, the wind dropping away to leave a gauze curtain of cloud, grey and forbidding, hanging motionless above Sourton Common and the surrounding Tors. I wanted to walk Walter's route to the peat works and picked up the trackway on the lane running alongside the Fox and Hounds. On the main road leaving the lane I turned almost due north and followed the track parallel with the river Lyd. To the south east, the grim outline of Brat Tor with Widgerys Cross just visible, glowered down through a soft tissue of mist. I turned my back on it and set off towards the north east, skirting around Great Nodden and inside Combe Down. The track grew steeper as I climbed and despite the mist that enveloped me in a cold wet shroud, I was warm and damp with sweat.

At the second bridge, built to span the Lyd, now unsafe and crumbling, the track doubles back to climb around the base of Hunt Tor, passing close to the Logan Stone and Great Links Tor, until finally it runs almost due east heading straight for Kitty Tor only stopping when it reaches the peat workings.

It was an eerie sensation standing in that desolate waste surrounded by the debris of what was fondly hoped would be a major Dartmoor industry. The earth was scarred where the workers' knives had sliced and opened up the turf in a patchwork of rich umber and black. A few rusting remains of old machinery stood amid the ruins of the old buildings. Inexplicably, the army were asked to blow up these buildings in 1961, as if attempting to eradicate all signs of this example of Dartmoor working history.

The cloud layer now covered the surrounding hills and Tors, settling down like a white quilt, cutting down visibility to less than fifty yards. Nothing disturbed the abnormal silence other than the murmer of water where the Rattlebrook commenced its life's journey. Not a bird sang. I was cocooned in damp white cotton wool, clinging to my anorak, my eyelids, my moustache, in tiny globules, isolating me from the world so completely I was compelled to walk to the remains of a wall and touch it, fearful that in losing my sense of orientation, I had also lost my sense of physical contact. No landmarks, nothing at all to assist my sense of direction or point the way home.

How often must Walter have found himself in this situation, but with the consolation of his workmates as company on the way down. My only consolation was the knowledge of the track, without it I would have been hopelessly lost. With it to guide me, provided I did not wander off, I should be able to find my way back to the main road. I left the peat works and began the descent, peering anxiously at the ground for the slightest change in texture from the broken hardcore of trackway ballast to the heather and bracken of the moorland surround. For this change would mean I was wandering off the track. This I did after crossing the bridge over the Lyd. Instead of swinging back and away to my left I continued straight on, losing my footing as the trackway gave way to the sloping hillside. Down I slithered and rolled until fortunately I landed almost on the track again where it had doubled back beneath me. I could hear the Lyd quite strongly now and the sound of that running water would continue on my left almost to the final turn off at Nodden Gate. It never entered my head that I could be lost or not be able to find my way down. I just plodded along, head down, enjoying the womb-like embrace of the mist, and the sense of total isolation.

Suddenly and in complete surprise, I became aware of lights. The changing beams of vehicles on the Tavistock-Okehampton road; the closer, and more inviting lights of the Fox and Hounds. I was amazed to find it was dark. Evening had crept over the moor. I could hear a car door slamming, voices echoing across the car park as the occupants entered the pub. I began to hurry. I was thirsty and needed a rest in front of the fire I knew would be blazing in welcome. On this occasion I believed I had earned it.

DARTMOOR REFLECTIONS: "I USE DARTMOOR AS I IMAGINE OTHERS USE UNIVERSITIES."

THE AUTHOR
AND THURBER

AT HUNTINGDON CROSS ON THE ABBOT'S WAY

FERNWORTHY RESERVOIR

DARTMOOR IN WINTER

KING'S TOR

Raven. 27"
from captive bird ♀ "pruk".
Powdermills. Sept 1975. Robin Armstrong

Silhouette of Raven
in flight

Buzzard profile for
Comparison

Bank vole. (Clethrionomys glareolus)
Powdermills. October 1975.

Otter (lutra lutra)
from mask. Postbridge 1926. June

DREWSTEIGNTON

DARTMOOR PONIES

FINGLE BRIDGE

A BIT OF DEVON THAT HELPED SPANNY SAVE THE NATION

POWDER MILLS

GILDERS HIKE AT THE DARTMOOR INN, MERRIVALE

VII

THE INNS OF DARTMOOR

The Inns of Dartmoor have played a great part in my life over the past years and I trust will continue to do so for many more. Many changes have taken place and I am not entirely convinced that they are all for the better. The motor car has assumed an importance and deference in the minds and attitudes of some landlords, showing itself in the 'modernisation' of the existing premises. This invariably means losing the Public Bar and its incorporation into the 'New' lounge, usually boasting a dining section.

I have no objection to families dining together in the beauty of the Dartmoor setting. It is a habit I indulge with my own family. What I do object to is there not being a bar where drinking men and women can sit, smoke, drink and talk in a genuine pub atmosphere, without the intolerable odours of frying fat accompanied by the continuous passage of 'Chicken in a Basket', or 'Scampi' under one's nostrils. For food frying and draught ale or bitter do not mix. There is nothing more calculated to spoil a fresh drawn pint of bitter than a pyramid of greasy plates containing a debris of soggy chips, chicken bones and soiled napkins placed alongside.

The other more damaging consequence of these renovations is the resulting loss of 'local' trade. The 'new look' no longer provides the convivial and restful atmosphere of the pub of old, where working men, tired after a day in the fields or quarries, sat and talked, played endless games of 'euchre' and put the world to rights. Their place has been taken over by the new

Dartmoor commuting fraternity.

'Well, old man, I worked it out. I can live here quite happily and still carry on with the old job. Of course it's lucky we have the branch in Plymouth. So I go there during the week and pop up to London on Thursdays. Back home here on Friday evening, so it all works splendidly.'

'Yes, I do the same. I've got it down to a fine art. I can leave Shepherds Bush at midnight and be home in three and three quarter hours. I do that every week in both directions. It makes all the difference with the new motorway. Life is so different here. The pace is so much slower, don't you think? I'm so relaxed all the time. Of course, it's wonderful to be out of the ''rat race''.'

They haven't 'got out' of anything. The 'rat race' is not some undefined, inanimate object. The 'rat race' is people. They bring the 'rat race' with them and dump it on our doorsteps. The 'rat race' is a mental acceptance of a way of life and the only way to escape is to completely change one's way of life. It requires a great deal more courage and effort than merely changing houses.

Fortunately, not all the Inns have been through this metamorphosis. There are still bars where it is possible to sit and listen whilst others talk, interrupting with the occasional question. Where concern over the inroads made by wild mink on the salmon and trout of the Tavy are of far more importance than the political situation. Where the necessity of planting potatoes towards the west if you want to avoid frost in late May is of greater concern than the minutes saved in frenzied dashes to and from London. Many of the people I drink with have never been to London, and yet they somehow manage to live their lives without any deep sense of deprivation.

I owe a great deal of my knowledge of Dartmoor and its working population to conversations in the many hostelries on winter nights with the steam rising from damp clothing, the atmosphere cloudy with tobacco smoke, and the talk revolving around where the best salmon are 'lifted' and which of that unique breed of Dartmoor poachers could be considered overall champion!

On just such a night, enjoying a reviving pint after a wearying day, I listened to five members of a farming family discussing a relative who had been found dead at his farm, curled up in his armchair before the long-dead embers in his large fireplace. He had died as he had lived for the last years of his life, unloved and alone. He had lain there for a week before anyone thought to see if he was alright. He was a wealthy man, a very hard business man, very rarely seen socially since his wife died, save at the markets where his only interest was in the price his cattle would fetch. As I returned home, I found myself thinking about his death and the sadness of his life. I tried to set down in a poem how I felt:

MOORLAND FARMER

He had been dead for a week when he was found.
A stroke,
Expected,
Surviving two that had left him pocketknife double
Without the use of one arm.
He had contrived
Since she had died
Years past,
To cook and clean for himself.
The farm-help seldom saw him
So hadn't asked,
And frankly didn't care.
The vet discovered him
Twisted up
In his dog-destructed chair.
They respected him,
The granite grim
Soul sad farmers.
Bearing his burden, body downwards to the Church
He had not visited since she was buried.
Arranged weekly flowers for the grave
And gave
Produce at harvest festival.

Careful,
Hard to best at a sale
But sound,
Could take his drink,
Without pushing to buy his round.
Always paid a debt
And yet
Spent nothing on the farm.
'It was good enough for my father and it's good
Enough for me'.
Accepting of course a grant
Or subsidy.
Hated politicians.
'Bloody fakes and charmers. Tell me, what
Has government ever done
For farmers?'...
Voted diligently
Tory naturally,
Hunted compulsively,
Shot pathologically
Anything that walked or flew,
Never knew why.
Never smiled,
Hardly ever talked,
Hard and unrelenting
As the granite ground on which his cattle walked.

EPITAPH
Here lies a moorland farmer
Contumelious and thrifty
Buried in 1971
Died in 1950!

The greatest change to affect the Inns of Dartmoor is
that of ownership. Almost all are Free Houses and as a
result, many are purchased merely as objects of speculation. The buildings themselves have more value than
the goods they once purveyed. One extremely well-
known House has changed hands three times in less

than fourteen months.

The consequence of this is two-fold. Firstly, it affects the local inhabitants who, having only the one House in the village, now lack a landlord who has any desire to integrate within the community. Secondly, it has meant the sad demise of the 'local' landlord, bred on the moor and thus understanding the nature and habits of his customers. The few that still survive have stamped their personalities and character on their surroundings and their Houses.

The thatched roof charm of the Drewe Arms at Drewsteignton holds a particular place in my affections, for it still retains all the characteristics of a typical Dartmoor Inn of a century ago. This is in no small way due to the presence of Mrs Mudge, better known to her regulars and locals as 'Aunt Mabel'. She has been Host here for fifty-seven years. Prior to this she spent three years at Crockernwell, a mere three miles away, so sixty years of her life have been devoted to serving others as a publican in this area. Here you will find none of the popular innovations considered so essential to the new generation of pub customers. The cloth-draped wooden beer barrels are still racked up behind the bar and from them emerges beer with taste and bite. It is even possible to order a pint of cider — a habit almost extinct in this county supposedly celebrated throughout the land for this beverage.

An evening at the Drewe Arms with its surrounding square of thatched cottages and fifteenth century granite built Church of Holy Trinity, is an evening well spent, in an atmosphere of charm and rural dignity of a bygone age, and no new visitor will leave without having paid for at least one pint of scrumpy for one of Mrs Mudge's celebrated regulars.

The Royal Standard at Mary Tavy on the Oke-hampton-Tavistock road lacks the architectural delights of the village square at Drewsteignton, but it boasts a landlord of the same character and service as Mrs Mudge. Bill Warne, the longest serving publican in the Tavistock area, is a celebrated local, respected and loved in the village. And like so many of the old Dartmoor publicans, rears cattle and sheep on the moor.

Bill's service to the community extends further than merely quenching thirsts, for he has inherited a gift that makes him invaluable to humans and animals alike. He has the power to charm away warts in humans and ringworm in cattle. I don't understand how he does it, but I have witnessed it. I took a young boy, with fifteen warts on one hand and thirteen on the other, to see him. 'How many warts have you?' asked Bill. 'And don't forget that a double wart counts as two.' He then lightly took hold of both the boy's hands. 'You don't want these, do you? Alright — they'll soon be gone.' And that was it. Nothing else took place, and no payment of any kind was allowed. Five weeks later the youth showed me his hands — completely free of blemishes.

In the same way, he does it with cattle. Farmers phone him and tell him the number of cattle who have ringworm. They receive the same replies that the boy had, and in some extraordinary manner, the cattle recover. Bill, who inherited the gift from his mother, can only pass it on to a female member of the family.

Should you be in the Royal Standard during the week of Tavistock's 'Goosie Fair', you may be lucky enough to hear Bill's wife, Mary, sing, in tones as clear as a bell, all the verses of the *Goosie Fair Song* and you will be privileged, for there are few people left today who can remember the words, or the tune.

If you would like to hear *Widecombe Fair* sung with its original tune and lyrics, or listen to the *Song of Dartmoor* rendered with verve and feeling, then go to The Tors at Belstone and with luck you will catch Bill Ellis, the Port Reeve, in good voice and comparable spirit, along with his friends, enjoying an evening in a manner Dartmoor men and women have done for years.

VIII

KING'S TOR

One of the pleasantest things in the world is going a journey; but I like to go by myself. I can enjoy society in a room; but out of doors nature is company enough for me. I am then never less alone than when alone.

William Hazlitt
On Going a Journey

My natural instincts have always been toward isolation. I do not fear loneliness; on the contrary I cherish it. Total freedom can only be realised in total isolation. Consequently, although I have a great many friends on the moor, I have not walked Dartmoor seeking companionship. Rather do I flee to it as a refuge against a surfeit of human involvement, my dog my only companion.

Life has taught me that whenever three or more people assemble together, one will always assume by divine right the mantle of leadership, a second will deny that right by virtue of a supposed prior claim. Both however, are united in their belief that the third has no right other than to obey their commands.

I am not a follower, neither have I any desire for power over my fellow man and I cannot comprehend the need and desire for it in others. I walk Dartmoor alone because in this manner all the decisions are mine. I go where I like, when I like. I do not require to convene and consult, blindly following my leader, aping the actions of sheep grazing the hillsides.

I use Dartmoor as I imagine others use or have used their universities. My head is master of my feet; my heart dictates to my body. To move on or to remain where I am is determined by my feelings of harmony with my surroundings. What can I possibly gain by relentless pressing forward when my present location still holds wonder and excitement, a catalogue of unanswered questions. If my brain has not been tested, my senses aroused, my emotions touched, then of what purpose is walking four miles or forty.

'Because it is there' has always seemed to me one of the most stupid reasons ever given for doing something. I do not walk Dartmoor because it is there, but for what is there, for the knowledge, pleasure, peace and joy I derive from my understanding of what is there. And if in so doing I make a new friend or meet an interesting acquaintance, then that is a bonus for which I am grateful.

Another bonus is the act of discovery; not the discoveries of an archaeologist, historian or geologist, but personal discoveries that at the moment of awareness seem of overwhelming importance, but eventually assume their own level of significance in a personal appreciation of the moor.

Such a discovery was my Holly Tree. The day I found it I had intended to walk from the lay-by on the main Tavistock-Princetown road above the river Walkham, near Hillside Cottage, and make for King's Tor. Here I would pick up the old railway track and follow it to Yelverton. I had calculated it would take me about four hours without hurrying to reach my destination.

It was a winter's day, cold bright with a pale sun offering a pretence of warmth. A day for walking and viewing, the air sweet and clear without haze or cloud, the surrounding hills and tors standing out in sharp relief against a pale blue sky. Thurber, bounding ahead, flushes out an enormous cloud of birds which, rising skywards, separate into two flocks, golden plover and lapwings. On the ground feeding peaceably together, they had intermingled into one harmonious congregation, but the moment danger threatened they fled with their own kind, all unity forgotten. I have noticed exactly the same thing in the fields around my cottage where fieldfare and redwings feed. Arriving and departing in separate flights, they search for food in one integrated flock without rancour or unrest, only danger divides them.

Climbing Long Ash Hill for less than a mile I reached the stone rows — a double line of standing granite running roughly east to west almost parallel with the Tavistock-Ashburton road. In the centre of the rows is a circle of raised turf with slabs of granite embedded in the soil. Surrounding them are hut circles and stone circles stretching from Long Ash over King's Tor and across Walkhampton Common. The sepulchral circles of Dartmoor, the Dancers of Stall Moor, Scorhill on Gidleigh Common or the Peter Tavy circle on Langstone Moor fascinate me. Why were they built? What strange compulsion drove primitive men or women, whose lives were lived in fear and hunger, to devote so much energy and labour — which could have been better spent improving their domestic situation — in raising monuments to baffle and bewilder the finest brains of future generations. Certainly the builders of these circles were not alone in their obsession with this shape; primitive cultures throughout the world have for centuries used it to express religious belief. For the American Indians the configuration of the circle played a fundamental part in their lives. Hehaka Sapa, or Black Elk, of the Teton Dakota, who fought at the battle of Little Big Horn and later toured with Buffalo Bill, wrote of the importance of the circle to an Indian:

Everything the power of the world does is done in a circle. The sky is round and I have heard that the earth is round like a ball and so are all the stars. The wind in its greatest power, whirls. Birds make their nests in circles, for theirs is the same religion as ours. The sun comes forth and goes down again in a circle. The moon does the same, and both are round.

Even the seasons form a great circle in their

changing and always come back again to where they were. The life of a man is a circle from childhood to childhood and so it is in everything where power moves. Our tepees were round like the nests of birds and these were always set in a circle, the nation's hoop, a nest of many nests where the Great Spirit meant for us to hatch our children.

> *In this circle*
> *O ye warriors*
> *Lo, I tell you*
> *Each his future.*
> *All shall be*
> *As I now reveal it*
> *In this circle;*
> *Hear ye.*

It is Dartmoor's affinity with other cultures, other civilisations, from time's beginning to the present day, that holds me spellbound. The ghosts that surround me people the landscape of my imagination. It is unimportant to me whether historians verify that the Menhir standing in front of me on the old Tavistock-Ashburton track, once a branch of the Abbot's Way, with a large 'A' and 'T' carved on the appropriate sides, was erected by monks. Facts are the food of journalists and politicians; imagination the drink of poets. I have never carried a copy of Hansard or a newspaper with me on the moor, but have drunk deep the draught of poets.

The romance of Dartmoor however, is always tempered by the realities of its past and these stone rows are a continuous reminder of that. During the time of the Great Plague the stone rows were known throughout the area as the Plague Market or Potato Market. Food and supplies were left here by the country dwellers of Dartmoor for the people of Tavistock, who were ravaged by the plague.

> *I see the tracks of the railroads of the earth,*
> *I see the menials of the earth labouring.*

I move on, leaving Long Ash behind, climbing towards King's Tor, crossing the Long Ash brook where it veers past the enclosure wall, and reaching the railway track, head towards the cutting. I never visit this section of the old G.W.R. branch line that ran from Yelverton to Princetown without a feeling of intense frustration at opportunity lost, and an awareness of incredible waste. I also count myself lucky to have been privileged to travel on this line from Plymouth when I was stationed in Devonport Barracks during the war and remember it with wonder as the most spectacular train journey I have ever made.

Today, what could have been a most successful railway line carrying nature lovers, tourists, walkers and day visitors into the heart of Dartmoor and thus alleviating the ever growing congestion of charabancs, over-large wagons and motor cars on its roads during the summer months, is a derelict ruin.

I walked through the cutting carved out of the slope of King's Tor whose granite rocks towered over me one thousand three hundred and fourteen feet above sea level. The track takes a tight left curve passing the ruins of a gangers' hut and a number of blackthorn trees still thick clustered with sloes, and I come out of the cutting into what was known as Royal Oak Siding, the junction to Swell Tor Quarry. Away to my left behind Swell Tor the line can be seen two hundred feet above, climbing past King's Tor Halt, rounding the southern slope of Hessary Tor and continuing on to Princetown.

In front, the line sweeps away in a series of curves. bending left to Yes Tor and sharp right around Yes Tor Bottom to Ingra Tor Halt. This halt was built for the sole purpose of allowing walkers access to an isolated area of Dartmoor and is surely the only station in Britain to have a notice warning travellers to protect their dogs against snakes. A very sharp left curve takes the line around Ingra Tor passing Routrundle farm on its right and Leeden Tor on the left. On — under Sharpitor, Leather Tor, crossing the Princetown road over a granite bridge on the slope of Peek Hill and dropping away towards Sheeptor and Burrator.

Close on my right a bridge crosses the old tramway built in 1823 to allow granite to be taken from Swell Tor and Foggintor quarries to Plymouth, in horse drawn trucks. The tramway was rebuilt by the G.W.R. in 1883 to carry steam engines and coaches. Alongside the bridge runs Royal Oak Siding where cut and dressed granite from Swell Tor was shunted on to the main line for transit. Not far from the bridge granite 'sets' have been piled into a wall, obviously to await loading on to a train that will never arrive. It's an extremely sad place, haunted by left over dreams and the tragedy of wasted manpower, wasted mineral wealth and wasted opportunity.

With a feeling of depression brought about by my surroundings I spotted my Holly Tree. Close against the bridge, sheltered by the bank as it sloped to the tunnel entrance, it stood strong and proud, its trunk bent slightly as a concession to the prevailing wind, its foliage thick and olive green and its head shaved where the wind cleared the top of the embankment. Its presence there affected me like a trumpet blast of pure joy; triumphant and alone it was a symbol of challenge. Seeded by the wind or carried by a bird, it flourished where only the blackthorn dared. Although Hucken Tor close by is lush with green, it's dwarf oak and mountain ash that cover these granite slopes down to the Walkham Valley, not holly, nor could you find another holly tree for miles around.

There it stood and still stands, for I visit it every year, defying the elements and making mockery of the cry that environment is the corner stone of survival. It has survived because it wanted to and not even the great blizzard of 1963 or the drought of '76 has caused it to deviate from its purpose.

Trees have always been capable of arousing emotional response within me. Some years ago I walked across North Africa and during an earthquake in Algeria worked for a relief organisation run by Abbé Pièrre. Our camp was pitched on a remote hilltop, bare of trees or green foliage, and every evening I walked down to a stream and sat watching the sun set behind a solitary poplar tree on a neighbouring hill. Not until it was dark would I return to camp. That lone tree was my salvation against the misery that then surrounded me and I shall never forget it. In like manner I never visit my holly tree without returning stronger in resolve and happier in mind.

It's a simple climb up the rock 'clitter' of King's Tor to the summit. From here the view is as fine as any on the moor; northwards across the Tavistock-Ashburton road, Cox Tor, Mid Staple Tor, Great Staple Tor with Roos Tor behind; looking westward, Pew Tor, Vixen Tor, and rising out of the Walkham Valley, the wooded slopes of Hucken Tor. Turning slightly NNE, Great Mis Tor dominates the landscape in granite capped glory.

Below, the hamlet of Merrivale is grouped around the road bridge, consisting of a handfull of cottages and the Dartmoor Inn. This inn was made famous by novelist and writer Eden Phillpotts, who named it 'The Jolly Huntsman' in his novel *The Mother*. There Samuel Bolt and Jill Wilket came with seventeen guests for their wedding breakfast and the hosts, the Toop family, served a breakfast of duck sufficient for an army. The whole of the action of *The Mother* takes place around the area of King's Tor. So much of Dartmoor can be learned and understood by reading Eden Phillpotts. I am amazed that he is so neglected today. Where in literature is it possible to find a finer descriptive passage of autumn than in the opening chapter of *The Mother — Falling Leaves?*

Now in wisps and canopies they leapt or fell, ruddy and pale. They flew by night or dropped heavily at the touch of still dawn's finger. The russet, the scarlet and the etiolate leaf, that had lived its little life in shadow, now came together and joined hands in a death dance; fell and flew and flitted and twisted in the gigantic breath of the autumnal equinose, gyrated upward on sudden whirlwinds in lonely places, and sinking at last to earth, yielded up their treasure in the alembics of the latter rain.

Only beech leaves and oak leaves, like weak souls, clung to dead joy and parent boughs that knew them no more. And it seemed as though the brown spikes that held next year's glory cried to them in the voice of the wind, 'Depart, ye auburn shadows and cease your sobbing, for ye also have won your meed of life's feast from earth and sky. The spring and summer hidden in time are ours. Therefore vanish and haunt the cradle of life with images of death no more'.

Looking down on Merrivale, it is difficult to believe that a few years ago a flourishing community lived there and in the surrounding area. Twenty-five families lived at Merrivale Cottages, pulled down to make room for quarry expansion. Further up the hill towards the quarry stood a Methodist chapel also destroyed. Hillside Cottage remains across the road from the Dartmoor Inn and is still lived in by Mrs Jeffreys who brought up her family there.

Towards Rundlestone were Red Cottages, Hill Cottages, Parson's Cottage and two large black painted houses — all pulled down, along with a second chapel.

Foggintor School and a school house that stood at the roadside between Rundlestone and Merrivale, built after the first world war to educate the large population of children living in the area, has also gone. Ceasing to have a function with the dissolution of the working community, the school was closed and the schoolhouse became a private dwelling known as 'Fourwinds'. This well built property was allowed to fall into disrepair. Travellers across the moor from Ashburton, Princetown and Tavistock watched in amazement and anger as the buildings gradually disintegrated and a demolition van took away what remained. Along with it went a wonderful opportunity to use the property for dedicated lovers of the moor. With easy access from the main road, surrounded on all sides by the most exciting and enjoyable of Dartmoor's walks, it was ideally situated as hostel accommodation.

It is always sad to see buildings left unused, in conditions requiring them to be demolished. It seems to me there is a basic flaw in the character of the rural property owner that continuously allows this to happen and nowhere is it more noticeable than on and around Dartmoor. In a country whose housing situation is as critical as ours, with little or no chance of it improving, any property left empty or neglected, capable of housing a family in need, is an affront to society.

Do you realise, do you realise, sir, what it means when you have nowhere to go? For every man must have at least somewhere to go.

Crime and Punishment
Marmeladov/Dostoyevesky

In their lifetime, my parents had 'nowhere to go' and awareness of this has affected me a great deal. My own cottage, the first and very probably the only property I shall ever own, or desire to own, has had a tremendous influence on my life. I cherish it and am acutely aware of my good fortune in possessing it. When I first discovered it however, it was condemned.

Some years after I had moved in and carried out a vast amount of work rebuilding and restoring it to its original condition, I was visited by a lady who asked if she might look inside. She stood in the centre of the lounge gazing around her. 'Isn't it quaint. You have done a lot to it. Fancy anyone wanting to live here. I used to own it you know. In fact,' (walking over to the window and waving her right arm around in a circle embracing the world), 'I owned everything around here the fields as well. Fancy you living here and doing all this work yourself.' She gazed at me with a look of charming condescension. 'I never did know what to do with this cottage. I finally decided to have it pulled down you know. Well, it wasn't any use to me, but still you have got it nice.' If ever this nation ceases to be a property owning democracy I shall not need to seek far for the reason.

It seems to be generally assumed that the families who left these Dartmoor cottages were pleased to go, glad to live in modern homes with the amenities of town life. Talking to them does not confirm this. Some would gladly return to their old granite built homes tomorrow — if they had not been demolished. They remember with joy the community spirit. Few complain of the loneliness or isolation, nor did they seem to find the Dartmoor winter difficult to live through. Anyone caught without sufficient food to live out a blizzard was considered a fool. Most recall with pleasure the dances and whist drives in the Community Centre and the joy of going visiting. Almost all attended chapel and agree that although times were bad, money scarce and work hard, they prefer the old way of life to the advantages of contemporary society. Those fortunate to still remain regret only the interference into their lives by official bodies on present day Dartmoor.

I wondered about the descendants of these people, now scattered, out of necessity, throughout the towns and cities of England, living in acre after acre of indistinguishable concrete wilderness, row after row of characterless Whimpey wonderlands, block upon block of towering monoliths reaching to heaven in soulless similarity. The dwelling places of giants for a race of pygmies.

I cannot believe their modern environment has in any way endowed them with more dignity or spiritual awareness, improved their relationships as human beings, advanced their moral or social values, or provided them with anything approaching the happiness enjoyed by their parents or grandparents who lived here in individual cottages, tending their own vegetable plots with acres of unspoilt moorland as their garden.

But me nor palaces nor satraps please;
I love to look on happy cottages.
The gems I seek are seen in virtue's eye;
These gauds disgust me, and I pass them by;
Show me a home like that I knew of old,
Ere heads grew hot with pride, and bosoms cold;
Some frank good deeds, which simple truth may praise;
Some moral grace on which the heart can gaze;
Some little hopes that give to toil its zest;
The equal rights that make the labourer blest;
The smile on which eternal love we scan,
And thank his Maker while we look on man.

Ebenezer Elliott
Philanthropist, Poet and General Reformer

Mrs Jeffrey's daughter Dorothy talks of her life at Hillside Cottage with obvious enjoyment and recalls the time she spent as housekeeper at Fourwinds:

'I remember preparing breakfast in the kitchen looking out of the window at the sun climbing above King's Tor, eagerly awaiting a glimpse of the first train from Princetown. Prompt at eight every morning it would come on from King's Tor Halt, puffing its smoke around the curve of King's Tor and, with a blast on its whistle, enter the cutting to be lost from view in Royal Oak siding. It was a wonderful sight.

'Fourwinds was a fine old house. It had running water in all the bedrooms, taken from Long Ash and run for about three quarters of a mile underground by pipe. I think the pipe is still there.

'When I was a child at Hillside you knew, I never saw my father for months at a time, except Sundays. He used to work at Burrator building the reservoir. He

would leave when it was dark in the morning and not
return until long after I was in bed at night. He would
have to walk from Merrivale to Burrator. The railway
was no use to him. He started work too early in the
morning and finished much too late at night. He
didn't follow the line; he would go over Vixen Tor to
Sampford Spiney and Walkhampton and on to Burrator.
It must have been well over ten miles each day and then
do a day's hard work in between.'

I was rudely awakened from my King's Tor reverie
by the sudden barking of Thurber, and going to
investigate, found her exultant over discovering a
pond about six feet wide and eight feet long in the
centre of a small plateau halfway down the clitter
overlooking Swell Tor. Unlike that on Over Tor, where
it's said a Mrs Bray washed her hands and earned it
the title 'Mrs Bray's Wash-hand Basin', this was not a
granite hollow filled with water, but a natural pond
obviously fed from a spring, for winter or summer I
have never found it dry. Many a happy hour have I
spent since, sitting with my feet immersed in the cold
water, the warm wind in my face, gazing down into its
depths, eagerly searching for signs of life, but alas have
seen nothing, although knowledgeable friends assure
me life must exist there.

This second discovery completed my day and I
decided not to continue along the railway line, but
return home by way of Swell Tor and Foggintor
quarries. The way into Swell Tor quarry is along the
rail back from the junction and the route is littered with
the remnants of its industrial past. Solid granite
buildings, capable of lasting out time, stand on the
right, requiring nothing more than a new roof and glass
in the window openings to make them usable. On the
left, a large stack of what seems to be Early Gothic
arches, about eight feet long, rebated in a series of
receding planes, obviously the remains of an order
never completed. There is sufficient 'cut and dressed'
granite here to build a large house complete with out-
buildings, and everywhere stacks of granite 'sets' are

standing, awaiting delivery.

Between the disused quarries of Swell Tor and Foggintor there are enough finished 'sets' to pave almost the whole of Tavistock town centre, yet I have no doubts there are a multiplicity of laws preventing anyone removing enough granite to build a chicken house.

The only active quarry left on Dartmoor is Merrivale, the workings hidden from sight across the road, with only the waste stone banking running from the Dartmoor Inn up the hill indicating its presence.

Some years ago I watched fascinated as heavy wagons drove away from the quarry, loaded high with granite that once constituted the greater part of old London Bridge. Bought by the Americans — it's generally believed under the mistaken idea they had bought Tower Bridge — the stone returned to its original home, Merrivale, to be re-cut and marked like a gigantic Leggo for re-assembly in Arizona. As these wagons turned right, heading for Plymouth, other wagons carrying the sawn flanged, rebated and polished balustrade for the new London Bridge, turned left and drove away towards Exeter.

In its original state in the quarry the stone is separated in layers on natural beds; these layers have a series of seams which are drilled for blasting, splitting the stone along the seams and jumping the block forward on its bed in one hundred, two hundred and three hundred ton sections. These sections are further cut by frame saws with ninety steel blades per frame, lubricated and assisted by steel shot, water and lime, cutting a three-quarter inch slab at the rate of half-an-inch per hour, roughly four inches per day. There is also a six hundred feet endless carbon steel wire, assisted by silicone carbide, running at sixty mph capable of cutting through four stone blocks simultaneously, at the rate of eight or nine inches per hour. Polishing is done by machines using steel rings with silicone carbide and finally felt pads and tin oxide.

The workmen are all highly skilled craftsmen, capable of working to extremely fine limits. The new London Bridge balustrade was assembled before transit and required no further alteration or re-alignment and was ready in every way for permanent erection. Many of the workmen I know. They made me a superb dining table in polished Scottish granite. Sadly, the quarry stands in the shadow of the official receiver. Should it close, it will end another source of employment on Dartmoor and leave the clay workers of Lee Moor alone, to continue centuries of working-class tradition.

Should you walk from Merrivale to Peter Tavy over Cox Tor, you may be very lucky, and pick up a track across the Tor marked by small stones. These were carried and deliberately dropped by quarrymen living at Peter Tavy to mark their way to and from work whenever mist or rain blotted the landscape from their view.

I picked up my track, running from Foggintor quarry to the main road between Fourwinds and Rundlestone, passing Yellowmeade farm. lived in for some generations now by the Cole family. This has always appeared to me a typical example of hillside farming. Clinging for life to the slope, carved out of the surrounding moorland, protected by a patchwork of walls holding back the ever encroaching heather, gorse and fern, it stands as a permanent example of agricultural determination. The very sight of it framed against the hill strengthened my own sense of purpose and with a light heart and a firm tread I took the road home.

IX

THE PAINTERS OF DARTMOOR

There is a pleasure in painting which none but painters know. In writing you have to contend with the world; in painting you have only to carry on a friendly strife with nature.

William Hazlitt

There is nothing more soul destroying than the sudden and absolute awareness of one's own stupidity, lack of understanding and knowledge. This awareness came to me at the age of twenty-five, soon after my arrival in London to work as stage manager/carpenter at the Intimate Theatre, Palmer's Green. My parents were variety artists and my education was undertaken wherever they settled, mostly during periods when they were out of work. For seven years in the thirties they scarcely worked at all except at odd weekends in working mens' clubs around Leicester.

I left school completely soon after my thirteenth birthday when my parents, one step ahead of the debt collector, moved to Lancashire. I went to work in a cotton mill which I endured until at sixteen and a half I volunteered for the Navy as a boy telegraphist. Demobbed a month before my twenty-first birthday, I resolved — like so many in the same situation — to do what until then no one had suggested we had any right to do — live.

Four years of total irresponsibility finally awakened me to an awareness of being an oaf, without comprehension or appreciation of what made life so excitingly worthwhile to others around me — books, music, poetry and painting. I became obsessed with the desire to learn, but every official approach for help met with refusal. It seemed I lacked sufficient education for further education and quickly realised I would have to teach myself. Fortunately, I was in the right place at the right time. London became my university, I haunted the National Gallery, the Tate Gallery, the Victoria and Albert and British Museums, soaking in everything they had to offer and all for free. My tutors were my friends — Edith Young, John Mellon, Gus Hickson, Brian Rogerson, David Nathan and later, Denis Wreford, and I eternally bless and thank them for their patience and understanding.

The City and Guild Art School at Kennington took me as a student providing I could pay my fees and keep myself alive. I obtained a job as a telephonist at Euston Telephone Exchange and managed to survive, working at night and attending school during the day, until offered the job as assistant to sculptor Benno Elkan, working on the Menorah, bought by the House of Commons and presented to the people of Israel.

Benno Elkan, a fine sculptor and a wonderful man, had fled to this country from Europe to escape the Nazis who, because he was Jewish, destroyed his public works in Austria and Germany. He knew Chagall and Kokoschka and their paintings hung on his walls. He talked lovingly about them and Winston Churchill, whose portrait he modelled in bronze and which was reputedly the only portrait Churchill ever liked. Through Benno Elkan I met Jacob Epstein.

Through my work at the City and Guild I came to know Augustus John who, although eighty, had just started modelling portrait heads and his work was cast in plaster by students at the school. I also met John Skeaping who was 'visitor' in sculpture and was at that time living in Chagford on Dartmoor.

These were good times for me; the doubts, uncertainties and fears of war forgotten, I settled down to try and compensate for the wasted and neglected years of my youth. It was not easy for I knew nothing and started from scratch, storing up knowledge like a squirrel and only much later was able to assess its actual worth and discard what was not required. As a consequence, my learning lacks discipline and I would give my left arm today — my right being required for serious drinking — for the privilege of a university place where in calmness and with willing help I could put that learning into some semblance of order.

However, these years were not wasted. Most of the friendships formed then remain and the love I acquired for poetry, music and, most of all, painting, is stronger than ever. This love intrudes into most aspects of my life, particularly that of walking. Whenever I walk on Dartmoor, observing its constantly changing moods — brooding cloud patterns, dazzling contrasts of light and shade, the pure cubism of its rock formations and bewildering complexities of its landscape — I am amazed it has never become a base for a school of painters.

> There is no juggling here, no sophistry, no in-
> trigue, no tampering with the evidence, no attempt
> to make black white or white black; but you resign
> yourself into the hands of a greater power, that of
> Nature, with the simplicity of a child and the
> devotion of an enthusiast — study with joy her
> manner and with rapture taste her style. The mind
> is calm and full at the same time. The hand and
> eye are equally employed. In tracing the common-
> est object, a plant or the stump of a tree, you learn
> something every moment.
>
> William Hazlitt

I have searched for painters using Dartmoor as inspiration and have been fortunate in obtaining help and guidance from John Skeaping's son, Nicki, who runs a gallery in Tavistock specialising in the works of such artists. With his assistance I have gathered together the names of a number of painters varying in talent and ability who have included Dartmoor in their work. Obviously there are others I have missed or have lacked space to include, but here you will find familiar names; and others less so, but all have found creative impulse in the landscape of the moor.

W.S. Morrish: born 1844

A Chagford man who painted in water colours and oil, and is still remembered in Chagford. He knew and loved the moor. At his best an extremely talented artist who lacked consistency. His son, B. Morrish, was also a water colourist but without his father's ability.

Philip Mitchell R.I.: 1814-1896

A self-taught painter in water colours. He painted West and South Dartmoor and the Tavistock area. He was a founder member of Plymouth Arts Club and the President. He finished his life near Tavistock and his work is now commanding national attention. A contemporary of Mitchell is John Barrett, a fine example of his draughtsmanship being in Plymouth City Art Gallery. He worked in oil and water colour.

Arthur Dingle: Thomas Dingle

Father Arthur and son Thomas Dingle, exhibited together in the Bath and West Society Exposition in Plymouth Arts Club, 1893, and in Fine Arts Exposition at St Andrew's Hall in 1877. Both were accomplished painters, senior in oil and junior in oil and water colour. The work of Thomas Dingle can be found in Exeter and Plymouth City Art Galleries. His style tended towards 'Impressionism'. His father was more Victorian and far less prolific.

G.H. Jenkins

Very little seems to be known about this artist who worked between 1890-1920, and was competent in oil and water colour. He is also known as a painter of coastal scenes.

92

Arthur Bevan Collier

Came from London to Bude and then moved to Sampford Spiney, where relatives still live. A prolific artist in oil. Also painted scenes of North Devon, the Cornish coast and South Devon as well as Wales and Scotland. Dates are not known, but in May 1908, one hundred and ninety-eight of his works were auctioned, presumably after his death. As a tenant of the Duke of Bedford it's known that his rent was one painting annually.

C.E. Brittain

A resident of Tavistock where he is remembered and held in regard out of proportion to the quality of his work, which I personally find without inventiveness.

William Williams of Plymouth: Born 1808 in Penryn

Always signed his work 'William Williams, Plymouth', although he was born a Cornishman and lived in Topsham where he died in 1895. A fine painter, both in oil and water colour in the Victorian tradition. His work now commands high prices and justifiably so.

William Widgery: 1826-1893: Born — North Molton

Lived in Exeter, well known around the moor for his paintings in oil and water colour: also painted coastal scenes. Not generally well known, was also a talented wild life painter and of sporting scenes. He was a prolific painter and the father of:

Frederick John Widgery: 1861-1942

Accepted by most people as the one 'true' Dartmoor artist, he developed a style of his own using gouache, which has been unsuccessfully copied by many painters since. Painted in oils using thick colour in his father's style. Illustrated many books on Devon and Dartmoor.

Other painters whose names occur occasionally with Dartmoor scenes are:

Samuel Prout: 1783-1852: A fine and important

Devon artist
William Payne: worked between 1776-1830: A fine
artist in water colour
John Wallace Tucker: 1808-1869: Exeter artist, very
good in oil and water colour
John White R.I.: 1851-1933: Devon artist
W.H. Pike: 1846-1893: A Plymouth artist in oil and
water colour: good
William Cook: circa 1832: water colours
F.J. Snell: 1860-1940: Water colour: inconsistent
S.G.W. Roscoe: Water colour: inconsistent

All of these artists have examples of their works in reputable galleries and exhibitions and are most sought after by collectors.

Contemporary painters seem to find little or no inspiration on present day Dartmoor and I am only able to mention two artists who seem to me to have captured and reproduced any of the spirit and feeling of the moor.

In 1974, an exhibition was held in Exeter Royal Albert Museum and Art Gallery of the work of Bryan Senior. He works in oil and acrylic and his paintings were undertaken in an area bounded by Haytor, Widecombe, Manaton and Yarner. Without in any way romanticising Dartmoor, he manages to capture its solitude and loneliness. By using the natural colours of winter — burnt umber, the orange-red of the bracken (in contrast to the wishy-washy mauves we are used to in the works of so many Dartmoor painters), the washed out greens and slate greys, and by isolating the single pony against the harshness and angularity of the rock piles, he conveys the timelessness and open hostility to the unwary of Dartmoor. He understands the movement of water and in *Becka Falls* and another extremely fine painting entitled *Cascade*, he reproduces the fascination that falling water holds for us all. Bryan Senior is a name to remember and I am convinced his association with Dartmoor will flourish and mature into a perfect artist/subject relationship in the coming years.

Finally, one of the most talented artists working in this country today, painter and sculptor R.J. Lloyd. Reg Lloyd was born in Hereford in 1926 but was moved to Dawlish at the age of two. He has lived and worked in Bideford for many years and become an accepted part of the North Devon landscape.

Lloyd's work is essentially his own; original in concept and execution and wide-ranging in subject matter, yet continuously returning to landscape and in particular the relationship of people in landscape. Here are not merely figures 'in' a landscape, but rather 'of' the landscape; interchanging forms with the undulations of hills or the standing stones of centuries, outlines softened by shadows cast by a climbing moon above distant tors, merging figures and landscape into integrated abstraction.

In gouache, oil and occasionally monotype, Dartmoor is illustrated in all its seasons and Lloyd has succeeded above all painters in capturing the complexities of its moods. The hardiness and hardship of its livestock brutally illustrated in paintings like *Ramshead*, and *Winter Sheep*, the isolation and loneliness poignantly observed in a pencil and wash drawing of Bowermans Nose, the dazzling scarlet of a warning flag superimposed against a winter sky in *Danger Zone*, or the brilliant contrasting of cloud and rock formations in *Below Kes Tor*, provide us with ample proof that Reg Lloyd has come closer to disclosing the 'secret' of Dartmoor than any other artist.

But oh! what opportunity has been wasted here over the past centuries. Where were the painters of feeling and understanding, capable of recording for us the lives and conditions of the workers of the moor. Was the prosaic theme of the labourer at work too audacious a subject to be attempted. Where are artists of the calibre and sympathetic awareness of Jean Francois Millet, who in a single gesture was capable of expressing the lives and characters of a by-gone generation, and in a charcoal line could make us appreciate working men's age-long struggle with nature. Were there not subjects worthy of permanent record in the solitary figure of the peat cutter, the warrener about his daily chores, the wall builders?

'The loneliness of earth and sky so rendered the more striking by the presence of a few living creatures, those solitary figures are all that speak to us of life in this vast landscape.'

It is still not too late for a painter with the heart and eye of Constant Permeke or Joseph Herman to explore the creative possibilities existing within the working community of Lee Moor — the drama and visual excitement of their china clay background.

X

HOW SPANNY SAVED THE NATION

The name of William Palmer is known to a handful of people in the area around Lydford and Okehampton, although many more would know him better by his nickname 'Spanny'.

I first met him drinking in the bar of the Castle Inn at Lydford. He introduced himself to me as the man who saved England. As his story unfolded, I realised that for lovers of tradition and believers in superstition, this is precisely what he did. Every tourist to the Tower of London who visits the famous 'Ravens' is a witness to Spanny's achievement.

Sixty years ago, the raven colony at the Tower had become extinct and only one bird remained. Legend tells that if this should happen the consequences are disastrous for the country, with periods of crisis and national disaster. The order was given, 'Find young ravens', and Spanny answered the call.

Close to Lydford is the village of Sourton and it was here the nation found the source of its salvation. Since the middle ages Sourton has had a quarry. In fact, Bridestowe, close by, was built from its limestone, which is one reason why many of its cottages are excessively damp. For many years the quarry was a thriving concern and the waste stone formed hills that have views over the rest of Dartmoor and away to the slopes of Exmoor.

The quarry was also a producer of lime for farmers. Enormous crushing machines broke up the stone, which was poured down chutes into ovens below. Large oven doors at ground level allowed the lime to be

loaded straight into horse-drawn carts and taken away.
The manager lived in a handsome house above the
quarry, with its own drive, a walled garden and a
splendid glass conservatory which allowed him to sit
in the warm, watching his men working beneath. The
house was sheltered by a copse of copper beech and
conifers. Today in true rural tradition it's a ruin and
the area belongs to the Devon Trust for Nature Conservation and has become a sanctuary for wild life, with
badgers living in the woods and kestrels nesting on
the steep cliff sides of the quarry — it's a joy to walk
through.

The quarry, like all quarries after their working life
is finished, filled with water and thus it was in the days
when Spanny was six years old, a local farmer collected
all the lads together to help him catch young ravens for
the Tower of London.

'Course he offered us something to help, 'twa'n't
much, but he had money. 'Twas a bit of an operation to
start with. You had to make sure you weren't going to
drive them out of their nests too quick afore us was
ready for 'em, d'you see. We worked in threes: first
three got hold of long kidney bean sticks and took all
the bark off: then we tied'm together in long lines and
pushed 'em out over the surface of the water till they
stretched from one side of the quarry to the other.

'The other lads then climbed the top of the quarry
above where the ravens were nesting in the quarry face
and started to throw small pebbles at the nests. The
young birds left the nests to avoid the stones, but could
not fly very far, not even the width of the quarry. Of
course they could see the sticks floating on top of the
water, for with the bark stripped they was white, so
they landed on top of the sticks. All us had to do was
slowly pull in the sticks, carefully lift off the birds and
put'n in a cage we had brought with us.

'Mind you, we had to be bloomin' careful 'cos the
quarry sides were very steep and you couldn't step in
the water for nobody knaw'd how deep 'twas. The
farmer, he was called Palmer too, wasn't no relation,

he sent us up his field where he had a bad sheep and we brought'n back, slaughtered'n and fed the young ravens on'n for two months, then we took'n to Bridestowe railway station and sent'n up to the Tower of London.

'We did this once a year until I was thirteen and my family left the area, so all they ravens at the Tower are descended from good old Devon stock.'

It was Spanny who told me about the Ice Factory and explained where to find it, declining however to walk with me to view it. I took the road from Bridestowe through Sourton leading to the Highwayman Inn and made this my starting point, on a miserable, cold, January day, with driving rain and sleet. I had a companion with me, who at the last minute declined the dubious pleasures of walking the moor in such conditions and elected to remain in the warmth of the Land Rover, at least until opening time.

Calling a reluctant Thurber, I crossed the Okehampton-Tavistock road and made my way past the fourteenth century Church of St Thomas of Canterbury, along the track over the disused railway bridge, and began the ascent of Sourton Tors. To the right, East Tor glowered over the main road, above and beyond Corn Ridge and Woodcock Hill with the valley between providing the source of the Lyd. Ahead, High Willhayes was totally obscured by rain and cloud and turning left Yes Tor similarly hidden from view. The rain whipped across my body, soaking deep into my clothing, my saturated woollen hat sponging a river down my back, bursting through the dam made by a knotted 'kerchief around my neck and flooding into shirt and vest. My ungloved hands were pitted blue with cold and I lost the feeling in my toes.

It never occurred to me to turn back. It did to Thurber however, who after trying twice to escape without my noticing, finally abandoned all pretence and deliberately ignoring me set off towards the Land Rover, turning now and then to gaze sadly back when I called, until a mere speck in the distance, she disappeared over the skyline. Even labradors have limits to their endurance and she had reached hers.

In normal conditions it's an easy climb up the Tor, although the slope near the summit becomes increasingly steep, but the boulders provide support and shelter from the wind. Below, running north to south, is King Way, a track that once formed part of the Mary Tavy-Sourton section of the old Okehampton-Tavistock road. Most of the track is indistinguishable, but it can be traced near Rattle Brook Head on the peat railway and again between Sourton Tors and the Corn Ridge, where it runs towards Iron Gates, the boundary between Sourton and Okehampton Common, on its way to Meldon. Here it is joined by tracks from Sourton and Southerly.

On this track I set course into the teeth of the wind, ice needles of rain puncturing my face, my boots ankle deep in sodden turf. I was engulfed by the desolation of winter, its dank, decaying odour filled my nostrils. Only the isolated blackthorn, branched mourning black, challenged and defied the elements.

> *Anti-social winter*
> *Coarse and crude.*
> *Lacking subtlety*
> *Indecent*
> *Rough and rude*
> *Why do you cling so tenaciously to life,*
> *Hold back spring's breath*
> *With*
> *Chilling visions of death's harvest.*
> *Unashamedly flaunt you skeleton limbs*
> *In cruel exhibition of our certain end,*
> *Leave us our dreams*
> *For these we comprehend.*
> *Taunt not with truth*
> *Why should we know*
> *What fate awaits us*
> *When it's time to go.*

Here were all the ingredients that tempt so many to describe Dartmoor as 'the last of the wild places'. I have never understood what was meant by this term. Dartmoor is where I run for refuge from the truly 'wild places' — the towns and cities of my daily life. The wildness that surrounded me was a pretence, a sham, an attempt to hide the truth from prying eyes. It was the wildness of imminent rejuvenation, a breathing space whilst the earth regained its composure, recovered from the rigours of its productive past and prepared for its creative future. These magnificent hills and tors, the twisting valleys where rivers run bordered by woods and tangled undergrowth, are not wild to me but friendly and tame, abundant with gifts from a bountiful earth.

Even the water seeping out of the ground from a natural spring could be put to practical use, and was, here at the ice factory on Prewley Moor. The site lies to the left of a row of standing granite posts, the widest apart, allowing King Way to pass between, known as 'Iron Gates'. The casual walker could pass the site without being aware of its existence or significance. All that's left are some man-made earth banks and a pit. These banks formed the sides of tanks flooded with water from a spring, each filled tank was sealed off and the water re-directed to the next tank. Four of these can be discerned at the site. The full tanks were left to freeze and the ice was then cut into blocks and stored in underground pits and huts, lined with peat and bracken for insulation.

With the arrival of spring, horse drawn carts transported the ice to Tavistock and Plymouth. Luther, a trawlerman I worked with some years ago, told me his grandfather who fished out of Plymouth, was one of the first to realise the benefits of taking ice aboard. He said, 'It came from off the moor near Tavistock and whenever he lost the wind he could ice down the catch and preserve it until landing. This meant longer periods at sea and more money.'

In a modern world where children make their own

'ice lollies' in the fridge as a matter of course, it's difficult to imagine how important the ice from this factory must have been to the lives of many people. Strangely, few if any writers about Dartmoor have considered it worth discussing. Crossing dismisses it in two lines and another book describes it as 'this amusing little industry'. Amusing! It would be difficult to imagine anything less amusing than earning a living on these bare slopes, rain slashed and frost coated, with soaked clothing and frozen limbs, cutting ice into blocks and burying it in the ground.

My own physical condition was very similar to that of those Dartmoor workmen, drenched and frozen, with one essential difference. I was here by desire and could leave whenever I liked. The thought of a warm drink, by a blazing fire and dry clothing, galvanised me into action down the final slope of Prewley Moor towards the track laid by the Water Board from the A386 to their moorland works. My legs were so cold that bending them was painful. Water from my sodden trousers ran into my boots squelching out through the lace holes.

Walking back to the Highwayman along the main road, I wondered about myself. Would I have the courage, however badly I needed money, to work at the ice works? The only conclusion I reached was to pray to God the circumstances might never arise that would force me to find out.

XI

POWDER MILLS

In October 1964, I was engaged in researching a film about Guy Fawkes and to glean relative information about black powder visited Powder Mills, the site of the old gunpowder factory that stands beside the Cherry Brook on the Moretonhampstead road between Two Bridges and Postbridge.

The area excited a tremendous interest within me, which I retain, and caused me for a short time, to go and live there. Then as now Powder Mills consisted of four cottages and a farmhouse with a large barn and a number of outbuildings. In the house lived farmer George Stephens and his wife. Their grandfathers had both worked at the factory, as had Mr Stephens' father. The whole area belongs to the Duchy of Cornwall and did in its heyday when it was a flourishing concern under the management of Mr George Frean, a Plymouth Alderman who founded the industry in 1844.

At its peak it provided employment for over one hundred workers, many of whom lived at Powder Mills in cottages since demolished. Others walked to work from Chagford, Moretonhampstead and Tavistock. It was a self-contained community with its own school, which partly remains as a shelter for cattle, and a chapel. Most of the skilled trades were represented among the workmen. There was a carpenters' shop, a blacksmiths' forge and a coopers' house, for the gunpowder was taken away by horse drawn carts in large wooden barrels.

Gunpowder was made from a mixture of seventy-five per cent potassium nitrate, fourteen per cent wood charcoal and ten per cent sulphur, the raw materials of which were ground down into extremely fine powder. This was done with large grindstones driven by water wheels.

The water source was the East Dart, along a leat across Chittaford Down close to Archerton, continuing on over Arch Tor to Powder Mills. The buildings that housed the wheels remain on the hillside, stepped one above the other, and their construction is a superb example of the mason's craft. A great many of the granite blocks used in the building are over six feet long, eighteen inches wide and two feet six inches to three feet thick. Also remaining are two chimney stacks that carried away dangerous fumes and sparks through underground flues from the buildings containing the powder. Even this precaution was not foolproof, for explosions occurred frequently blowing off timbers and roofs.

The powder was used for blasting in the quarries of Devon and Cornwall. Its strength was tested in a mortar standing on the track to the farm; the distance the mortar fired a cast iron ball determined the strength of the powder. That it works I have proved, for at the end of the film we held a firework party at Powder Mills which the Stephens attended, along with a host of children, and as a fitting climax we fired the mortar. To the intense joy of all present the iron ball travelled nearly twenty feet.

Powder Mills is magnificently situated as a centre for walking, surrounded by landscape of fascinating aspect and historical incident. Crockern Tor frames the west side, with its southern slope running down to the main road above Two Bridges. It hardly looks significant enough to have become the centre of a power struggle between the House of Commons and the Stannary Parliament of Dartmoor. Yet here, after the dissolution of the Joint Stannary Parliaments of Devon and Cornwall in 1305, the Parliament of Dartmoor tin miners met from September 14th 1494.

Standing on its windswept, boulder strewn summit today, it is almost impossible to imagine ninety-six miners crouching, shoulders hunched against the wind, around a large flat granite slab table, listening to the Elder seated in the Judge's Chair (a granite boulder, hollowed into chair shape by the elements), discoursing on Stannary Law. Or that by the reign of Henry the Eighth they would be so powerful that when Richard Strode, MP for Plympton, introduced into Parliament a bill concerning the silting of harbours, which considerably limited their working rights, they ordered Strode. to appear before them on Crockern Tor, and that when he refused, had him arrested and flung into Lydford Keep, the Stannary prison. There he languished until obtaining release by posting a one hundred pound bond with the deputy warden of the Stannaries. Only upon the approval of Strode's Act in the House of Commons, did that House establish its supreme power over the Stannary Parliament and thus point the way to its eventual demise.

The last Stannary Parliament met on the Tor in 1749 and thereafter assembled in Tavistock. Today even the enormous granite slab table and Judge's Chair have been removed from Crockern Tor and only the story remains.

From Crockern Tor, northwards along the valley of the West Dart for two miles, is Wistman's Wood, a high Dartmoor woodland of stunted, twisted oaks, covering eight acres of clitter covered hillside. At one thousand two hundred and fifty feet above sea level, buffeted by high winds, often blanketed by thick cloud and subjected to an average rainfall of seventy inches per year, grow pure pedunculate oaks, many five hundred years old, none taller than twenty feet and often with a spread of twenty-five feet. Tightly packed together, their branches block out the light creating a great humidity beneath, ideal conditions for lichens, mosses and liverworts and the ferns growing in the forks of the trees.

The gnarled trunks and branches, interweaving

leaves and boughs, and dense undergrowth, make this a place of wonder and awe and given to tales of mystery and mythology. Consequently, it is visited by an ever growing stream of tourists and this very interest could ultimately change the pattern of its growth, for their presence has opened up gaps through the foliage to the sky and the resulting sunlight is killing off the undergrowth.

A permanent feature of Dartmoor are the leats, covering the landscape in all directions, some still in use, others abandoned. In the fringe towns, Ashburton, Buckfastleigh, Sticklepath, the leat water was used to power woollen mills and drive the grinding stones of corn mills. On the moor they were pot-water leats for farms or used by the miners as a power source for the crushing, washing and smelting of ore.

By far the most interesting leat, particularly for the walker, starts here in the valley between Beardown and Longford Tors. In 1793 the Plymouth Dock Waterworks Company was granted rights to take water from the streams of the Cowsic, Blackabrook and West Dart and carry it to Devonport, thirty miles away.

The West Dart leat leaves the stream above Wistman's Wood on the slopes of Beardown Tors and runs parallel with the river, but stays above it falling gently with the contour of the hill. On Beardown Hill it goes through a weir in a conifer wood and emerges in the fields above Beardown Farm. Originally, the leat turned west here, doubling back along the Cowsic valley to join the River Cowsic leat at its weir. Today the Dart water runs into a pipe that carries it over a stone aqueduct to join the Cowsic leat and together they flow under the Two Bridges-Tavistock road and head towards Princetown.

Close to the prison walls the leat turns south and crosses the Blackabrook, which becomes its third source and the now complete Devonport leat makes its way past Tyrwhitt's Tor Royal House and heads for Peat Cot. Peat Cot is a nineteenth century settlement and was part of Sir Thomas Tyrwhitt's agricultural dream. To the south of it lies White Works, named after a mine worked by Moses Bawden of Tavistock. Between White Works and Fox Tor to the southeast is a flat waste known as Fox Tor mire, one of the few really dangerous bogs on the moor.

The leat makes a half circle at Peat Cot, curving around the contour of the hill, past White Works towards Nuns Cross. Here it meets its first serious resistance, the high granite bed stretching between the rivers Dart and Meavy. The leat cannot go around, so it goes through, disappearing into a tunnel for six hundred and forty-eight yards, emerging from a beautiful stone arch in a deep bed below Nuns Cross.

Nuns Cross or Siward's Cross, is the first mentioned cross on Dartmoor. It is named as a forest bondmark by the perambulators of 1240, but most likely was in existence long before this. About a mile and a half from the Cross eastwards across Nuns Cross Farm and Ford, towards Sand Parks, there is a cairn, a stone circle and a kistvaen, close by a small cross about four feet high and two feet across set on a rock. This is Childe's tomb. Allegedly the grave of a wealthy Plymstock landowner, caught hunting on the moor in terrible weather, he slew his horse and disembowelled it hoping to stay alive by crawling inside. Unfortunately he froze to death. He 'ordained by his will that wheresoever he should happen to be buried, to that church should his lands belong.' This story is excellently told by Crossing in his *Guide to Dartmoor*.

After leaving Nuns Cross, the leat has a three mile journey towards the Meavy valley, past more stone crosses, and Crazywell Pool on the heathland under Cramber Tor. Should you be passing Crazywell Pool on Christmas night and a voice cries out your name three times — then tremble, for your time is up and you will depart this world before twelve months are past.

Past Raddick Hill about a quarter of a mile from the stone rows of Black Tor, the leat turns south to run down the rocky hillside of the Meavy valley, plunging in a waterfall one hundred and fifty feet to the Meavy aqueduct and continuing on under Leather Tor, until disappearing finally almost alongside the old Princetown railway track into a pipe to Burrator reservoir.

This is a fascinating walk, incorporating all that is best in Dartmoor's history and scenery. Surrounded by stone capped tors, in total isolation except for the plaintive squeak of a buzzard calling its mate, the rising of a lark, a dipper skimming the water, the glimpse of a solitary teal, and if the walker is very lucky, the sighting of red grouse — although I have never managed to see any. And always the leat, telling its own story: the brilliance of the surveyor, the craftsmanship in its construction and ever needed repairs and maintenance, the perpetual clearance of starwort, pondweed, water crowfoot and the reeds or bog grasses from its banks and bed.

The walk takes one a long way from Powder Mills, but it is my association with that site that opened up this area to me, and other areas also.

Leaving Powder Mills one full-moon bright, frost heavy, winter night, warmed from within by a surfeit of good cheer and good companionship, I set out to walk to Beardown Man. From Longford Tor the moon-raked mica, sparkling and glistening on Beardown, Crow and Higher White Tors, combined with the frost blanketed earth and the beamed reflections in the waters of the West Dart river, to create a jewelled paradise, a silver encrusted panorama of breath-taking beauty. The same that caused William Browne, the Tavistock poet, to write of it:

Hail thou, my native soil, thou blessed plot
Whose equal all the world affordeth not!
Show me who can so many crystal rills,
Such sweet-clothed valleys or aspiring hills,
Such wood-ground, pastures, quarries, wealthy mines
Such rocks in whom the diamond fairly shines.

What passed between the granite man and me, that winter night, remains my secret. Towering above me, his age-worn stone presence, awe inspiring in the moonlight, dominated the surrounding tors. The shadows and enclosing rocks his followers, loyal and protective, encircling me, menacing, silent. Devil or God, I bared my soul to him and emptied my heart and then, chastened and exhausted, walked home. I have never been back.

Because of Powder Mills, I obtained the wild life illustrations in this book, the work of Robin Armstrong. I first met him at Powder Mills after he had taken over the Stephens' farmhouse when George Stephens retired. A Londoner by birth, Robin Armstrong acquired in childhood his love and understanding of nature and an ability to reproduce it in line.

A solitary man, but not lonely, his natural instincts surround him with all the company of the countryside. His own high critical standards often force him to destroy the results of weeks of dedicated work. Working without help other than from friends on the moor in times of great need, he has persevered in his chosen profession and is finally receiving due recognition. Examples of his work can be seen in galleries and private homes throughout the south west and his talents are in great demand.

In Robin's company I have learned country lore; watched trout who thought they were unobserved and safe in the quiet places of the Cherry Brook; gazed spellbound at a buzzard's nest with young, in the topmost branches of a lofty Douglas Fir; caught rabbits, with dog, ferret and snare, and on a hot August afternoon, been fascinated by the antics of a family of mink playing in the shallow waters of the upper Tavy. At that time experts were assuring us there was no possibility of mink breeding in the wild and they had not become the menace to Dartmoor wild life, particularly salmon and trout, that they are today.

We have spent memorable nights together in the remaining Dartmoor inns where drinking in convivial company is still encouraged. He has introduced me to moorland people I now call friends and from their

friendship I have gained much. In this manner I came to
know Jack Price and through him, his father Harry
Price.

One of the most celebrated of all walks on Dartmoor
is that beginning at Fingle Bridge near Drewsteignton
continuing along the bank of the river Teign, along
Fisherman's Path before turning right to climb around
Hunter's Tor to Hunter's Path, passing the grim
granite arrogance of Castle Drogo on the left and thereafter dropping steadily down to Fingle Bridge again.
It's a walk of roughly four miles encompassing a
breathtaking variety of scenic beauty. At river level the
path runs through oaks coppiced by the monks of Buck-
fast Abbey, who forced the oaks to grow tall by planting
birch between. Every part of the tree was used, the
bark for leather tanning, the small twigs and branches
for charcoal and the boughs for wood. Every twenty-
five years they were cut down to allow their pole like
branches to grow from the stump. Today, sadly, many
urgently need replacing. Higher up, the woods are oak
standards, birch and plantations of conifer. On
Hunter's Path the walker hangs four hundred feet
above the Teign as it winds through a gorge that
began life four million years ago. Here also you are in
the presence of monuments from the Iron Age. Prestonbury Castle on Prestonbury Common between the path
and Drewsteignton is an Iron Age hill fort with an
inturned entrance leading to a triple enclosure with
wide spread ramparts. It can be approached on the
Drewsteignton road from Preston Farm. This fort in
common with two across the river from Prestonbury,
Cranbrook Castle and Wooston Castle, were not built
to defend the moorland peoples from invaders, but to
prevent them from invading others.

Fortunately these warlike propensities no longer
affect the moorland dwellers and the traveller can rely
on help and hospitality. Never more so than when, the
valley walk over, the visitor enters the Anglers Rest at
Fingle Bridge for the first time and meets Jack Price.
Inside decorating the walls are superb examples of

trout and salmon. Touch them, go on, there's no glass protecting them. Each one is a unique example of the creative genius of Harry Price. They are brilliantly carved out of wood and painted with such skill that seasoned anglers seeing them for the first time believe them to be real. On the shelves behind the bar other examples of his work are displayed. A leopard sprawls along a branch, tail swishing; below, gazing malevolent eyed at the watcher, a peregrine falcon poised ready for take off, bright eyed and alert, menacing the intruder with a weapon-like beak; or a long eared owl silently contemplating the inanities of modern existence. All this and much, much more, made up the life of Harry Price. If you are very lucky and happen to be the only customer, then ask Jack if you can look at his father's book. This book demonstrates for me the true greatness of the man. It is a record of a voyage around the world made in 1901 by the Duke and Duchess of York, later King George V and Queen Mary, aboard the Ophir and Harry was a member of the crew. Written in perfect script, every page illustrated with expert paintings of happenings aboard and ashore, it is a work of great artistry and craftsmanship and one day surely must be published so others might have the pleasure I had in reading it; and if you can finally persuade Jack to tell you his father's story then this will be a walk you will surely never forget.

'My father came from a family of Masterbuilders in Birmingham. He didn't want to be a builder, he didn't really know what he wanted. For two weeks he studied at Birmingham School of Art. In those days if you were good they moved you up a form, so in a fortnight he went right through the Art School. They told him they couldn't teach him any more. Finally, at sixteen he ran away from home and joined the Navy as a boy seaman on July 27th 1895 and eventually came to Devonport.

'It was at Devonport he realised here was everything he had been searching for, Devon, Cornwall, the open countryside and in particular, Dartmoor. He spent every leave and all his spare time walking Dartmoor. He loved it intensely, exploring every foot of it and attracting a lot of attention in his Naval uniform.

'I always remember him telling me how he first discovered this valley. He arrived one Saturday evening, walking down the valley, and stopped at the weir-pool when he saw the fish. His family were noted fishermen in Birmingham and he always carried a coiled set of fishing lines and tackle. Taking out his gear he started fishing, very quickly landing a couple. With a fire burning he wrapped them in dock leaves, then in grass, placing the wrapped trout in the red hot embers of the fire to cook. When done, he removed the charred grass, peeled off the dock leaves — the skin coming away at the same time — leaving the white flesh of the trout. There is no finer eating in the world than fresh caught trout wrapped and cooked at the side of the stream. By the pool with the evening sky blood red through the leaves of oak and birch, he made up his bed amongst the grass and fern and with the gentle murmuring river soothing him, slept.

'Early next morning he made his way to Fingle Bridge which he didn't know existed of course; he always found his way although he had no maps. Fingle Bridge then was even lovelier than today. Crossing the bridge he took the road to Drewsteignton and as he turned the corner at the bottom of the hill the church bell started ringing. At that moment he realised this was the place, this was to be home. He felt the pull of Fingle Bridge so strongly he knew he would make his life here. Although he continued travelling the world in the Navy, he always came back here and on leaving the Navy in 1907, he settled in Drewsteignton. He met my mother here as a young girl and although he was much older than her, he said: ''I saw this young girl and decided to wait for her until she was eighteen.'' She used to help her mother who traded around this area, eventually settling on a permanent site here where the Anglers Rest is today.

'My father had this great love and understanding of

nature. I learned my natural history from him. He would take me along the river bank and just by looking into a pool he would say, "There's a salmon there". He could read the tracks in the bed of the river and from these signs he knew how long the fish had been there and the size of it. I can do it — he taught me. He never caught a fish that he didn't eat. If it was a particularly fine specimen he would carve it to the exact size, paint it and hang it on the wall. It's wonderful watching the visitors when they see them. I've had wood carvers here who close their eyes and just run their hands over the fish. They say this brings the fish alive. Glass would only act as a barrier. They do the same with the animal carvings.

'I always remember my father with great love and affection. He was a wonderful man; a man of the countryside, a fisherman, naturalist, painter, wood-carver. He also had mechanical skill. His motto was "If it can be done, I can do it". He gave me knowledge and understanding of what life is all about. He is responsible for me living in this glorious valley and I'm eternally grateful. Many visitors say, "You don't know how lucky you are living here", but I do, oh yes! I do indeed. I wake every morning with that knowledge. I see the sun through the trees, hear the woodpecker hammering, the hum of bees and above all the sound of the river. If someone turned the river off in the middle of the night, I would know and wake immediately.'

Go to Fingle Bridge, walk the valley paths, open your eyes to the visual splendour that surrounds you and after, relax with a drink at the Anglers Rest and allow your hearts and minds to absorb the peace and understanding Harry Price bequeathed to his son, and that Jack Price now holds in trust for all of you. If, when you leave, you do not feel better equipped for life's struggle, then there is nothing free this world has on offer capable of giving you satisfaction and joy.

XII

HOW WE OPEN THE MOOR FOR VISITORS
EVERY YEAR

The letter arrived one morning in February and as soon as I unfolded it I realised the moment I had anticipated so eagerly for so long had arrived. For some the final accolade of acceptance by the community in which they live is becoming a member of the Round Table or the Rotary Club, Conservative or Socialist Club, or perhaps the Golf Club. For others it's being picked for the local football or cricket team. For me it meant none of these things; this letter and its contents was all I required. It was a simple letter with a bold black heading:

The Gilders and Colts:
Headquarters: Cornish Arms, Tavistock.

Dear Clive,
    On Sunday, 7th March, the Gilders Hike. We would like the pleasure of your company.

0900	Muster at HQ in full marching order complete with mid-day meal.
0930	Follow the standard to Merrivale. Compass will be swung at Wilsetton Cross.
1200	Customary ceremony by the Chairman, and procession through the Bishop's Way.
1215	Cross the Treasurer's hand with £5.00, or have your fortune told free.
1300	Meal may be taken without being fined.
1330	Last drinks at Treasurer's expense.
1331	Drinks from now on at your expense.
1415	Bus will arrive for those not wishing to hike. Those who wish to hike, make own way to Peter Tavy, where bus will be waiting.

1830   Reception at the Brentor Hospice by Squire.
        No ceremony.
1900   Hot meal.
2130   Make tracks toward 'ome.

Yours faithfully,

Tom
Secretary

'The Gilders and Colts' of Tavistock was formed over fifty years ago by a handful of Tavistock men who made a habit of meeting together on Sundays and walking the moor, with the intelligent object of arriving by twelve noon at the open door of an Inn. It was a gathering of friends who enjoyed each other's company, loved and understood Dartmoor and appreciated the therapeutic qualities of a pint of good ale. From these beginnings sprung a Tavistock institution that flourishes today, but whose objects remain exactly the same as those founder members still active will testify.

'We are Seven' is the motto on their coat of arms proudly displayed in H.Q., on their lapel badges, and there are seven Gilders, and that was the original number; today they boast a second 'Seven', the Colts — a shadow cabinet that duplicates in responsibility and authority the duties of the Gilders.

There is an overall President, aloof from both Sevens, a Chairman, Treasurer, Standard Bearer, Navigating Officer, Wine Steward, Minister of Transport and Secretary, each member with a duty to perform and a deputy to observe and assist.

Already however I sense your growing concern with this impressive display of official positions. You're dying to ask: what do they do? Why, bless your heart, they don't do anything, that's the sheer blinding joy of it; you become a Gilder or Colt because you love life and because it gives you pleasure to see others enjoy themselves. When did you last receive an invitation that had the word 'pleasure' on it? In this computer-

ised, standardised, depressingly bureaucratic land of
ours, is that not reason enough? Mind you, should
enquiries be made in and around Tavistock concerning
their activities you would be astounded at the positive
help, financial and otherwise, they have given the
community over the years. They will deny it of course.
It's against the rules to discuss it, so keep it to your-
selves or I won't be asked again.

The Gilders Hike always takes place in March and
this was a typical March day, blustering winds, rain
and very cold. H.Q. is warm and friendly, full of
Gilders and Colts and invited guests. Many I know well,
others through their professions, and some I meet for
the first time. Builders, drivers, publicans, members of
the local Constabulary, owners of shops and business-
men, all gathered together to walk the moor.

Good mornings are exchanged, caustic comments
fly back and forth concerning the confusion of walking
apparel particularly hats. Deerstalkers, cheese cutters,
trilbies, peaked caps that demand whippets to justify
their existence; checks of such dazzling squared
brilliance they should never be worn without 'band
parts'; woolly hats of all sizes, shapes and dimensions,
plain, striped and rainbow coloured with bobbles and
without, perched jauntily on the back of the head or
pulled right down protecting ears and nose, knitted by
loving hands still abed — no fools they; the Wine
Steward sports a Texas stetson so wide four of us could
shelter beneath should it snow.

Last second topping up of flasks is undergone and we
are ready. Standard Bearers to the fore, 'Follow the
Banners' is the cry and we are off down the Plymouth
Road, past the Bedford Hotel where breakfasting
guests rise from their tables gazing wide-eyed in
wonder as we pass. Up the hill to Down Road and
Whitchurch Down, leaving the hard roads behind
crossing the most beautiful of golf courses, passing
early morning golfers who wave us on our way; past the
Club House, built on land that belonged to farmer Jan
Doidge who at 81 still farms the area. Should you meet

him in the Club bar he will recount for you the story of how at eighteen months he was stolen by gypsies and later abandoned in the middle of the Princetown Road to be found by a travelling horse-drawn coach. 'They stole me to improve their breed', he says but he does exaggerate a little.

The rain has turned to sleet and the wind blows it into our faces; the party has stretched into a long line covering the skyline. The banners still flutter bravely ahead blazing the trail.

At Wilsetton Cross, the leaders halt allowing the main party to catch up and the Navigation Officer to swing the compass, an enormous wooden replica of which he wears around his neck. Furtive fumblings in hip pockets are followed by coats drawn across faces as life giving liquid is forced down throats — to be caught imbibing incurs a penalty fine. In the midst of this activity an altercation breaks out between the Navigation Officer and the Wine Steward concerning the route and speed of progress, which point is settled by the Wine Steward removing his stetson and beating the Navigation Officer around the ears with it, our enjoyment of which is ended by a shout and a pointed indication that the sky on our route ahead is clearing and patches of blue are appearing.

With renewed energy and purpose we continue on our way, taking the track past Hecklake with Pew Tor on our left, passing Heckwood Tor and halting again at Heckwood quarry for reasons of physical expediency and relief; carrying on to climb around Vixen Tor making for the Tavistock road above Merrivale Quarry and with the sun now shining overhead, descend the hill to the Dartmoor Inn.

Perfect planning ensures we arrive three minutes before opening time and we await the ceremonial entrance. The doors open and the landlord carries out a tray on which is placed a silver tankard full of ale. The Chairman empties the tankard and enters the Dartmoor Inn. We follow closely behind, down through the lounge and the Bishop's Way into the Public Bar.

The passageway between the lounge and the public bar in the Dartmoor Inn was named Bishop's Way by the Gilders on the 1st March, 1950, whilst on their annual hike and alterations to the Inn were taking place. One of their number, nicknamed 'The Bishop', took up a sledgehammer and struck a blow destroying the wall separating lounge and public bar; a proclamation was read and that same document now hangs on the wall of Bishop's Way.

Standard Bearers and Navigation Officer can relax; responsibilities are now in the capable hands of the Wine Stewards who ensure the whole company are supplied with liquid refreshment at the Gilders' expense until 13.30. At 13.00 the pasties, all home baked and carried out to the Inn by the coach party, are handed around — to be caught eating before this time would incur another fine. A great deal of the financial success of the Gilders can be attributed to these fines for in a spirit of low cunning the reasons for being fined are never explained until after payment. Undemocratic I agree, but the Treasurer thinks it a splendid system.

Warmth and good cheer spreads like a blanket over the bar; old friends no longer able to hike arrive to talk of passed walks, visitors inquisitive as to the nature and purpose of our gathering become new friends and throughout the Wine Stewards hover like predatory crows ready to pounce at the first sign of an empty glass. All too quickly it is 2 p.m. and we muster outside for the second stage of the hike. The coach party now grows considerably, but the rest of us set off along Pork Hill to round the bottom of Cox Tor and head for Peter Tavy. The resolution and vigour of early morning is noticeably missing from the party as we climb around the lower slopes of Little Staple Tor and head for the track between Cox Tor and Cox Tor Farm. In less than three miles we are strung out in small groups across the moorland, the two banners superimposed against the chilled blue of the winter sky from which the sun has withdrawn behind Cox Tor. Each party seeks out the easiest route but all are determined to reach the

Peter Tavy Inn. Stops for conflicting reasons are now far more frequent, strides so firm and decisive this morning now waver slightly as feet inexplicably and repeatedly point in opposite directions; occasionally a group will pause to assist to his feet a member who through reasons of extreme tiredness brought about by overwork during the preceding week, has desired a short nap in the bracken. Then, wonder of wonders, caught by the wind a large balloon-shaped object slowly rises above the skyline and moves away towards the west, gathering height and speed it spins like a U.F.O. finally setting course and direction towards Tavistock. Beneath and behind, losing ground by the second, comes a roaring, stumbling dervish, a stetsonless Wine Steward plunging faster and faster in hot pursuit until in a convulsion of arms and legs he sprawls across a clump of gorse and pitches over and over downhill to land spreadeagled and spent against a wall, and the valleys and tors resound to the joy of it as picked up from party to party, the cheers and laughter echo around and life is splendid.

From here on the going is easy. Youlditch downhill all the way, past Harragrove on to Higher Churchtown and finally the Peter Tavy Inn and tea. A roaring log fire awaits and a genial landlord and his wife provide a tea of scones and butter, cream, strawberry jam, layers of cake and gallons of hot tea which, suitably embellished, tastes like nectar. The coach party are already engaged in a card school in one corner and we are entertained by a talented singer musician who, to the disgust of the Wine Stewards, does not know *Eskimo Nell*. A raffle takes place for an expensive wrist watch and after it has been handed back three times to be raffled again, the fourth winner is ordered to keep it, consequently dropping it on the Delabole slate floor — presumably to test its shock proof qualities — and shaking head and watch together announces: 'It seems to have stopped working'. At the landlord's request and expense we have 'one for the road', and muster for the final stage of the hike.

Already we have walked over ten miles and at least a third of the walking party include men old enough to have retired from work and we still have a fair distance to go. From the Inn we take the lane past Gatehouse Farm, picking up the track running between the river Tavy and Longtimber Tor, following it to the bridge and from there climbing up to Mary Tavy, passing the Church of St Mary where in the peace of the churchyard lies William Crossing who lived in Mary Tavy for a period of his life and whose *Guide to Dartmoor* is a master work of Dartmoor literature. Finally we arrive at the Bullers Arms on the Tavistock road out of Mary Tavy. From here the remainder of the party will finish the journey by coach. Mike and I decide to walk; three others have already gone on ahead and we continue into Mary Tavy, along the main road before turning left at the garage and with Blackdown on our right head for Brentor. Above Blackdown, Gibbet Hill looms menacing in the gathering dusk and we leave the road down the track towards Wortha Mill Bridge, crossing the railway line that once ran from Tavistock to Exeter and provided one of the loveliest journeys in the land and whose lines were torn up with such speed it was obvious our masters realised it would become urgently required again in the future and were not prepared to withstand argument concerning it. After half a mile the track veers away to the right towards North Brentor and Mike and I take to the fields which rise quite sharply, leaving me to puff and pant behind. The climbing moon illuminates the outline of St Michael de Rupe, St Michael of the Rock, standing on the summit of an extinct volcano 1,130 feet above sea level with its west front a mere five feet from the cliff edge. Thirty-seven feet long, fourteen feet wide, it is the fourth smallest complete Parish Church in England. I was fortunate once to be passing the Tor on a summer's day and a wedding party left the church to descend the hill. The bride's white veil and dress billowing in the gentle breeze, the attendants in fresh spring colours all silhouetted against the church and sky, left an unforgettable memory. Now we keep the church on our left and climbing the last bank see the welcoming lights of the Brentor Inn ahead of us.

Journey's end, and nothing left ahead but good food, drink and excellent company. Inside all is warm and friendly. The table ready, we take our places for dinner. Toasts are drunk. Absent friends remembered. We wallow in recollections of past walks and walkers. Speeches are made and thanks given. Faces which earlier in the day were whipped into a rosy glow by the actions of the wind and rain now glow from within. We laugh together at everything and nothing, nudging and pointing at each other in good humour and affection, the most trivial remark causing paroxysms of laughter and applause. And then, quite suddenly, it is all ended. A last drink around the fire in the lounge; shouted goodnights to and from the landlord and we are aboard the coach for home. The Gilders Hike is over for another year and Dartmoor is officially open to visitors.

It is now yours. Enjoy it, explore and appreciate it. Love and cherish it; treat it with respect for we all hold it in trust for generations yet unborn. And if the Gilders' love for it and my words concerning it have still not convinced you of its value and worth, then listen to the words of the man who began this book, written over thirty years ago.

It would be much the best thing if you were brought up in the country. But it will be a very different countryside from that in which your father was brought up. People used to think that the big cities offered the fullest kind of life, and pleasure in abundance. They used to flock to them like pilgrims to a feast. But now these cities have brought death upon themselves and women and children have fled from them in terror. The age of big cities on our continent seems to have come to an end. This flight from the cities will bring tremendous changes to the countryside. The tranquility and remoteness of country life were already being undermined by the advent of television, the car and telephone and by the spread of bureaucracy into practically every department of life. And now that millions who can no longer endure the totalitarian claims of city life are flocking to the land, now that industries are being dispersed in rural areas, the urbanising of the countryside will proceed apace, and the whole pattern of life there will be revolutionised. The village as it was thirty years ago no more exists today than the idyllic isles of the southern seas. Much as he needs solitude and peace, a man will find them very difficult to come by.

Dietrich Bonhoeffer

FACETS OF CRIME

introduced by Ronald Duncan 11 photographs Price 95p
Eleven famous crimes and court-room dramas — ranging from murder to mutiny,
and robbery to rape, written by a team of well-known writers.
". . . a gripping collection of the changing face of crime."

Bill Norville, Bristol Evening Post

". . . a fascinating, wide-ranging anthology of crime . . . and with enough question-marks to trouble the reader long after the book is put down."

BBC Radio

MURDER IN THE WESTCOUNTRY

introduced by Colin Wilson 16 photographs Price 95p
Ten famous murder cases
"This murderous excursion from Bude to Bristol and beyond is recommended as compelling reading."

Colin Haxton, Southern Evening Echo

". . . unfolds ten tales of death and destruction . . . every murder throws up so many questions."

Charles Anderson, Western Daily Press

A MEAL FOR ALL SEASONS

32 illustrations Price 95p
Contributions by Angela Rippon, Rita Tushingham, Marika Hanbury Tenison,
Joan Bakewell, Joy Pardoe, Jane Toplis, Zyna Rossiter, Margo Maeckelberghe,
Ann Taylor, Audrey MacGilvray and Jean Tangye.
". . . recipes that are well worth trying."

Monica Mawson, London Evening News

"Exciting recipes, spiced with fascinating anecdotes . . . a real insight into the lives of well-known people living in the Westcountry."

Peggy Archer of the BBC

BOTH SIDES OF THE TAMAR

Devon & Cornwall portrayed in words and pictures. 24 illustrations. Price 95p.
Chapters by John Betjeman, Charles Causley, J.C. Trewin, Clive Gunnell, Tom
Salmon, E.W. Martin, Bill Best Harris, James Turner, Jane Toplis and Arthur
Caddick.
". . . a memorable book on Devon and Cornwall."

Western Morning News

". . . a dazzling array of talent."

Arthur Venning, Editor, Cornish & Devon Post

FOLLOWING THE FAMOUS IN CORNWALL

with chapters on D.H. Lawrence, Humphry Davy, R.S. Hawker and Others by
Michael Williams. 28 illustrations. Price 60p.
". . . a literary man's original and quite illuminating guide to that most magical of counties . . ."

John Theobald, Editor, Western Independent

". . . novel and appealing . . ."

Methodist Recorder